Miss Bangkok

MISS BANGKOK

Memoirs of a Thai Prostitute

by Bua Boonmee

with Nicola Pierce

In the interest of privacy, some people have been given pseudonyms. Any resemblance to persons living or dead is purely coincidental.

PUBLISHED BY MAVERICK HOUSE PUBLISHERS.
Maverick House, Office 19, Dunboyne Business Park, Dunboyne,
Co. Meath, Ireland.
Maverick House Asia, Level 41, United Centre, 323 Silom Road, Bangrak,
Bangkok 10500, Thailand.

info@maverickhouse.com
http://www.maverickhouse.com

ISBN: 978-1-905379-43-9

5 4 3 2 1

The paper used in this book comes from wood pulp of managed forests. For every tree felled, at least one tree is planted, thereby renewing natural resources.

This book is dedicated to my children.

ACKNOWLEDGMENTS

I WOULD LIKE to thank my children, my mother and my sister, for giving their love when I needed it most.

Thanks to my friends, especially *Roj, Priew, Parn*, and *Off*, for helping to make my job more bearable.

My thanks also to Nicola Pierce and Pornchai Sereemongkonpol for their great work in helping me to tell my story, and to Jean, Gert, Jessica, and Bridgette at Maverick House Publishers.

PROLOGUE

SOMETIMES I FEEL like a turtle that is being grilled over hot charcoal. I am slowly dying. No matter what I do, no matter how much I try to escape, I cannot. I am powerless to change my destiny.

I wonder was I born to be unfortunate; is this life my destiny? I pray to Buddha that this not be the case. My life seems to be that of a country girl who has spent her days escaping from a tiger, only to be eaten by a crocodile. Mine is an ever-worsening tale with no end in sight.

You see, I am a prostitute, though *farang*s prefer to call women like me 'bar girls'. I believe the term is more acceptable to westerners' ears. But to a girl like me, it is all the same.

My job means nothing to me anymore. I have long since given up any hope of happiness.

I exist for the pleasure of others. You might say the only certainty in my life is uncertainty.

I couldn't tell you how many men have bought me, not that it matters. I prefer not to remember them.

In Thailand, we do not talk about such private matters. It is not customary to talk of things that should be forgotten. It is also of little concern to a girl of my standing. The only thing that matters is the baht that I am paid.

Though I suspect that mine is not the worst existence in the world, I must confess I wouldn't know if it was. I know of little else.

You can buy me for 2,000 baht. In return, I will do almost anything that is asked of me, but I won't kiss customers—some things are just too intimate to do with a stranger. Kissing is for a wife or girlfriend; sex is for Thai girls like me.

CHAPTER 1

IF WE WERE to meet, you might comment on how I look slightly different to other Thai women. You might say that my face is round, like a full moon in the sky. This is a trait I inherited from my father, who was born in Ubon Ratchathani, the second biggest province in Isan, the northeast region of Thailand.

Bordering Laos and Cambodia, Ubon Ratchathani was the location for an American airbase during the Vietnam War. This may or may not have had something to do with my father becoming a soldier in his teens. By the time I came along, he was a sergeant major, responsible for the instruction of new recruits.

My father was a restless young man, or so he would later describe himself. When I was a little girl, he used to set me on a *krae* (a low table of bamboo) and tell me about how he had ended up in the province Nakhon Ratchasima, commonly called Khorat, where he was entranced by a beautiful young girl who worked at one of the stalls in the marketplace.

I have a black and white photograph of this girl, my mother, which was taken shortly after they met. Her oval face is framed by her shiny, black hair, which is parted in the centre and drawn up into a perfect bun on the top of her head.

She is wearing a sleeveless, V-necked, polka-dot dress, and is smiling sweetly at the photographer—in a way that only lovers do. She used to boast to me about all the men that flirted with her. She was proud of her beauty, particularly since she had to quit school in third grade because her family were poor farmers. Sadly, they saw no reason why a woman should be educated, only to be married off to a man and be dependent on him for the rest of her life.

I do not know what year they met, or what year they married. Little details like that have never interested me. All I know is that my brother Nop was born in 1973, I was born in 1974, and my sister Nang in 1975. Apparently we lived in rented accommodation for the first two years of my life. It was a tiny house of which I have absolutely no recollection, although I do remember my mother pointing it out to me one day. She tried in vain to jolt my memory about the room in which I slept and where my brother and I had played and fought together.

'Don't you remember that room, where you slept in a hammock as a baby?' she asked.

She also pointed out a tamarind tree, which she said I used to cling to when I was learning to walk, but I stared at it disinterestedly; it was a stranger's house to me, with its simple two-storey style and wooden fence.

'Sorry, *mae*. I don't remember it at all,' I replied, and she seemed a little disappointed.

After the arrival of the children, the rent got too expensive for my parents and we moved into accommodation in Khorat provided by the army. We lived there with other soldiers and their families. I think *mae* must have missed the little house, though she never admitted it; it represented more than simply being the first place she lived in after she married. It reminded her of a young couple in love and excited about their shared future. At least, that is what I like to believe, considering how the future unfolded.

The wooden town house that became my home was provided by the Thai government for its military. Accordingly, there was nothing distinguishing about it. It was one of hundreds that were built in small rows around the airbase where my father was stationed.

Each row consisted of ten columns for ten families, and each dwelling was a copy of its neighbour; two storeys with a small kitchen and bathroom at the rear and a bedroom/living area just inside the front door. Upstairs, there was another small bedroom and a tiny area in which to meditate and worship.

My father was the only one who used this room, and only on *wan phra*, or what you might call holy days. It had a little altar where a small Buddha sat, flanked by two vases of flowers.

Even now, I can still remember the heavy perfume of the incense sticks he burned as an offering to Buddha. The combined smoke of the incense and candles swirled as my father, kneeling in front of Buddha, chanted in a language unintelligible to me. I walked on my knees and sat quietly behind him in a position called *wai*—head bowed and hands pressed together—hoping that goodness would protect me. I remember that room as being filled with serenity.

Although we were poor, I didn't have an unhappy childhood. We grew up surrounded by tanks and military aircraft, which were of no concern to us children, though I have pleasant memories of watching planes taking off every morning.

The army base was a place where everyone knew everyone else. The women knew each other, the children knew each other; you could say that even the dogs were familiar with each other's tails.

Today, what I remember, perhaps more than anything else, is the colour of the earth. It was a reddish brown, and when you rode at full speed on a bicycle, the dirt would swirl up and taint your socks. It was contrasted by the surrounding greenery and deep-blue sky.

There were lots of trees and acres upon acres of green Bermuda grass. The summers were always extremely hot, and I can remember that the trees gave us shelter from the sun when it reached its highest point in the sky. A little bit away in the distance was a big, white wall that encircled the camp, shutting out the rest of the world. I am now a mother, and I realise the camp was perfect for children, who were unable to escape and always happiest when a parent was within shouting distance. The army base was our world. I had no inclination to leave it and explore what lay beyond its walls. You could say that I wasn't a very adventurous child, because I dared not leave the confines. Was this my first mistake—to ignore the bigger picture and be content with what was immediately in front of me?

ONE OF MY earliest memories is that of my mother getting me ready for my first day of school. I remember sitting on her lap as she gently braided my hair. I loved my mother, but if I had to choose which parent I was closest to as a child, I would have to say my father.

Por used to let me accompany him when he cycled to the market and also when he went fishing. The two of us would sneak into a paddy field where he'd dangle a bamboo stick that had a furiously wriggling worm or a small toad hooked to the end of it. He found it more productive to leave the stick unmanned for about thirty minutes or so and then return to check on its progress. I always hoped there would be a huge fish waiting for us, but invariably it would be just a little eel or a snakehead, which was better than nothing, I guess. My father would shrug in resignation as he pulled up the homemade rod, seemingly content just to have something to bring home to my mother.

Another highlight, if you could call it that, was the Red Cross Fair, which took place every winter. We went as a family, I holding *por*'s hand, my brother up on his shoulders, and *mae* holding my sister. These fairs were a marvel to me, with so many different toys on sale. Looking back now, I suppose it was just a few makeshift stalls selling cheap toys, but my brother and I were practically speechless with the excitement of it all. One year I fell in love with a blonde-haired doll and dragged *por* over to where she was on display, so he could admire her as I did. I didn't ask my parents for much as a rule, but I begged my father to buy her for me. He shook his head sadly in reply, 'I can't afford to buy her because if I buy you something, then I will have to buy your brother and sister a toy too, or it wouldn't be fair, and I just can't.'

I remember that day clearly because it was then that I learned that not everyone is equal. I watched other children leave the fair with their new toys, and I experienced envy, perhaps for the first time.

Por hadn't exaggerated. My parents never bought their children toys. My sister and I often collected leaves and branches to play make-believe *kai kong*, in which we would act out the roles of food vendor and customer.

My father was an honest man, and I believe he hoped that we would make something of our lives. Unfortunately, a soldier's lot was not a profitable one. I think he earned, at the most, around 580 baht a month, which was not enough to support a family of five. I now understand that's why the government provided free housing to soldiers.

New Year's Day, which was celebrated in one of the fields at the base, was the only occasion I would receive toys. All the children would line up, and the high-ranking officers would present us with a gift. I still cherish the memory of the day I was given a small doll and a box of cookies. It probably doesn't sound too exciting now, but we were poor and looked forward to such rare treats immensely.

Por was a quiet man who wanted a quiet life, but sadly, life in our house was rarely so. It was for this reason that he discouraged us from playing with the neighbouring kids. Sometimes, if one kid beat up another, the parents of both sides foolishly got involved and quarrelled. Although Thais generally try to avoid confrontation, as this is deemed as losing face, if a member of their family gets into a row, taking your family's side is a must, regardless of the circumstances.

In Thailand, it is customary not to lose face. Face is an often misunderstood part of Thai culture. It means, to put it simply, a state of being respected by others, and yet there is nothing simple about face.

Thais generally tolerate poor service, because to complain would mean to lose face, both for the customer and for the waiter. Although face was extremely important to the families in the camp, they still engaged in these petty confrontations.

The many similarities between the lives of our neighbours and my family, strike me now as being most peculiar. Children were driven to school on a bus provided by the army. Our fathers went to work and then returned home in the evenings to gather at bamboo benches under the trees to drink. Meanwhile, the wives developed gambling addictions brought on by boredom, and fought with their husbands for not earning more money. It was a demoralising life for the adults, though the children did not realise this until they were much older.

YOU COULD SAY that my parents were conservative. My mother was very disciplined when it came to her children, and spent a lot of time yelling at us not to do this or that. She never let me go downtown with my friends because, she told me, it was a waste of time, since I had no money to buy anything.

This was the one aspect of my childhood that I hated above all: the constant reminders of my father's financial predicament, particularly in relation to school. I can remember one time in particular when I wanted more than anything to be someone else. One of my school teachers told the class to make a pair of maracas out of two coconut shells. He wanted us to lacquer and decorate our instruments as colourfully as possible. He urged us to try our best, warning us that we were being graded on them.

That evening I went home and made a hole in the coconut shells, filled them with pebbles, and pushed a stick into each one. I shook them and they sounded like maracas. After playing with them for a while, I was ready to move on to the next stage—decoration.

There was nothing in our house suitable for this, so I asked *mae* for money to buy colouring pens and lacquer. She said no. I went to *por*, and he also refused, explaining that they couldn't afford it. There was nothing to be done except present my maracas as they were. I tried valiantly to trim the hair with the kitchen knife, but it didn't improve the overall effect; they were still very obviously coconut shells shoved onto two sticks.

The next day I brought them into school and nervously made excuses for the absence of any colour or frivolity. Instead of being angry, the teacher told me that he completely understood my situation, since none of the other poor students could afford to decorate their maracas either. He went on to say that, unfortunately, he couldn't give me a good mark for the assignment, because I hadn't completed it properly.

I do not pretend that this determined my eventual destiny, but I reacted to it by somehow admitting defeat. Today, I still think about this incident and how it affected me. I accepted what the teacher said and decided that there was no point in me trying too hard in the future, as I couldn't change my circumstances.

Poverty became a constant theme in my education. If we were given school projects to complete at home, I never asked my parents for help or money. Instead, I would tell the teacher that I was incapable of completing the task.

Such incidents had a profound effect upon me. Above all, I promised myself that if I ever became a mother, I would make sure my children never had to go without, and that I would do whatever it took to provide for them.

I WAS 17 years old when I first discovered that my father was unfaithful to my mother. I have no doubt that *mae* probably knew that it had been happening for years, but she never complained. That is the Thai way of coping with such problems. We avoid confrontation and decline, politely of course, to discuss issues that impact upon us.

On paydays, the men headed to a nightclub downtown where they discreetly flirted with women. Maybe it was their uniforms, or the fact that so many went drinking together in a jovial group without their wives, but whatever the reason, there was no shortage of extramarital relations. The wives never accompanied their husbands to the bars. It was strictly a male 'bonding' exercise, and they were a secretive bunch, protecting one another from disgruntled wives, providing alibis, and so forth.

Perhaps *mae* realised this a few years into the marriage, and turned elsewhere for excitement, but in a different way to my father.

The women at the base gathered in each other's houses while the men were at work. They spent their mornings doing housework and met in the afternoons to play cards and gamble. Normal practice was to return just before the husbands finished work, though my mother grew more careless about this as the months passed.

Gambling is a common enough source of entertainment in Thailand. Many Thai men bet on sporting events, from boxing to cock-fighting to *pla-kad* (fish-fighting), whereas the women gamble on card games.

Rummy was *mae*'s favourite. I wished that my mother wouldn't gamble so much, as we were constantly in debt. The women didn't play for big amounts of cash, but when you lost as often as she did, it began to add up.

You should know that I never saw my father with another woman during my childhood. I did, however, witness the disintegration of my parents' marriage. This was a slow and hurtful period of my life, one that I have since tried to forget, using the medicine of alcohol.

The frequent arguments were the first indicators that something was wrong. As a little girl, I found my parents' fights distressing. Even today I hate any kind of confrontation and always fear that a row will lead to physical violence.

Whenever my parents quarrelled I would hide out at a neighbour's house, and when a fight broke out there between the husband and wife, I would return to the safety of my own house. I couldn't bear to see people losing their tempers with each other. At least my father never hit my mother; some of the other kids I knew weren't so lucky. After a bout of heavy drinking, the wives—especially those who had gambled that day and incurred debts—would be left black and blue by their enraged husbands. The evidence was plainly visible the following day when these women returned to gamble some more, sporting black eyes, cut lips, and broken teeth. In our house it was different and it was *mae* who frequently thumped *por* during their rows.

Mae was spending more and more of my father's small wage paying off her gambling debts, and naturally this was a source of frustration to them both. She berated him bitterly for not earning more money, and he rebuked her for wasting the little money he did have. At the end of each month she would ask him for money, and more often than not, he had nothing to give her after settling his debts from the previous month.

He was never going to earn any more than he did. He had had a bad fall before I was born, and broken his leg. I loved to run my finger along the scar that stretched from his knee to just above his ankle. It reminded me of a centipede. He had needed a metal plate inserted, and as a result, he failed the medical exam he had to undergo in order to be promoted. However, he didn't seem particularly bothered by this, which probably angered my mother more than anything else.

A man of simple needs, he could never be accused of being ambitious. He enjoyed his army life and drinking with his buddies. None of his three children got to know him very well, or maybe there wasn't much to know.

One day I asked *por* for money to buy a snack, and he showed me his empty pockets. I got mad at him and asked him why he gave most of his money to my mother since he knew where it was all going. He looked at me and said, 'How can I refuse her when she insists?' How indeed!

Por managed to keep us afloat by borrowing money from his senior officers or from welfare programmes for soldiers. He borrowed to buy luxury items like a little black and white television set and a motorbike. There were only two TV channels, but it became an important part of our family 'quality' time. More importantly, though, it helped him gain face.

Gaining face is done by displaying wealth, so even poor people like my father would rather borrow money to buy luxury goods, and gain face, than do without.

Fortunately, *por*'s bosses charged a much lower interest rate than the loan sharks. Those 'official' money lenders were bad news, and many a family found themselves squeezed mercilessly within their grip when, inevitably, they couldn't afford the inflated interest, which only ever seemed to increase.

We always ate dinner together, sitting in a circle on a thin mat. *Mae* placed a few Isan dishes in the centre, and each of us had a small basket made of woven bamboo strips with a lump of sticky rice in it. The men and women sat together on the floor, the men cross-legged and the women with their legs modestly tucked to one side. It was fun when each of us tried to spoon up food while avoiding arm-clashing. My father would try to entertain us by bragging about how he tamed the new resentful recruits and bossed them around. As I grew older, sadly we ate dinner together less often.

Once my brother, sister, and I finished our homework, the TV was switched on. We watched cartoons, the news, and soap operas until our bedtime. My mother always got worked up during the soaps and would become impatient if she felt that the leading lady wasn't sticking up for herself against the vixen who wanted to steal the leading man from her. Every evening she threatened to beat the living daylights out of these bad women.

There's an exception to every rule and not all the families in the base were the same. There were just a few families who I thought were 'proper'. The husbands didn't drink too much, and their wives stayed away from the gambling parties. At the weekends they would pack up their cars and head off on trips with their lucky children. I longed to do the same with my own family.

It became a big issue for me that *por* never took us away for the weekend. A family that took holidays together seemed to me to have it all—money and the ability to enjoy each other's company. When these families returned, I would quiz the kids on what they had done and what they had seen, and then select the highlights to tell *por* in the hope of persuading him to bring us away the following weekend.

Our family never seemed to have any fun together; tension over money was a constant undercurrent in most of our interactions with one another. *Por* rarely watched TV with us. When things were bad between him and *mae*, as they usually were, he went drinking with his buddies in the evenings and didn't come home until we were in bed. He wasn't a heavy drinker, though—let's face it, thanks to *mae*'s hobby he couldn't afford to be. It was just easier to be with his friends than to come home to a frustrated wife.

SCHOOL FAILED TO save me, or maybe I failed to be saved by it. I attended primary and secondary school in downtown Khorat. All the kids on the base travelled to school on our own school bus. It was a long day, from 8am to 4pm. The primary school was an unattractive concrete building. Every morning at 8am we lined up in front of the flagpole to sing *Pleng Chad Thai*, the national anthem. I enjoyed the hour-long agriculture lesson in the afternoon, where we were taught how to plant and grow our own vegetables. We even made our own fertiliser from weeds and dead leaves.

Other than that, though, I'm afraid I wasn't a very good student, and rarely scored more than a pass mark in any of my subjects.

The English class was a particular source of terror to me. Each day we were given ten new words to learn for the next day's class. The teacher would then begin each class by having students recite their words individually, and I never failed to make a mistake. I hate to think that I was just a stupid child; perhaps it was my painful shyness that prevented me from succeeding at the task.

The teacher lost her temper with me one day after I stumbled and stammered over the words for ages. This usually sedate, middle-aged, bespectacled woman actually threw the blackboard brush at me in frustration, just missing my head by inches. My classmates were as shocked as I was as she yelled at me and angrily shooed me back to my seat. Imagine that! I was so stupid I had caused this woman to forget herself.

Back then teachers were still allowed to hit their pupils. We had to respect them as if they were our second set of parents. Today things are different; teachers can't physically harm students, but they might occasionally tap them smartly to embarrass them.

I was shaking for ages after I sat down, but she wasn't finished with me just yet. She asked the class to read aloud from the textbook and then hovered near me so she could hear my inevitable mistakes. How could I concentrate on what I was reading when I was busy praying that she would just leave me alone? She pounced on me and started jabbing me in the head with her finger, 'Can't you remember how to pronounce that? Can't you remember anything I've taught you? *Or have I been playing the fiddle to a buffalo?*'

To my horror I felt my eyes well up with searing hot tears as the cockier of my peers began to giggle at my ignorance and discomfort. Being compared to a buffalo is one of the greatest insults in Thai culture. That was when I made another promise to myself: never to cry, or feel sorry for myself. I was going to get on with it, because that is what life is all about.

I was fortunate enough to have a lovely teacher when I was 13. She seemed to really care about the students and wasn't interested in abusing her position as a figure of authority. Her classes were more serene. She always began them with a joke in order to settle us, and sometimes she would choose a lucky girl whose hair she would braid during the lunch break. She was a good listener, and if any of us had any worries, we found ourselves airing them in class under her gentle probing. I used to wonder if things might have worked out differently for me had she been my teacher all through my schooling because I was a timid child who couldn't function under duress.

Though I was a very quiet student and never misbehaved, the teachers mostly scared me, especially the ones who couldn't believe that I hadn't retained any information from the previous class. At times, I was so terrified of saying the wrong thing that I would actually freeze when picked on to answer a question—nothing would come out of my mouth, even when I knew the answer, and the teacher would tut-tut in disgust and move on to someone else. When I didn't understand something I dared not ask for fear that the teacher would scold me for not paying attention in class.

Students had to pass an entrance exam in order to be accepted for secondary school, and I will never forget the day the results came out. I was convinced that I wouldn't get in, but nevertheless I prepared myself as best as I could and took examinations in the subjects of English, Thai, science, and mathematics. It was an anxious wait for the day when the list of triumphant students would be made public. It was also my birthday, which made it all the more dramatic.

Early that morning *mae* took me down to a roadside spot where the monks from our local *wat* usually walked by, on their morning rounds to collect offerings from the villagers. My mother and I were going to 'make merit' and add to our karma account with an offering. I was excited because I rarely did this. Our family didn't have much to offer anyway. The sun was still orange as a line of monks appeared on the horizon. They kept a distance of several metres between them as they walked.

Each monk was accompanied by a *dek wat*, or temple boy, who walked behind him. Some of these *dek wat*s were children whose parents left them in the monks' care because of poverty—the same way people left their unwanted dogs at the temples. I couldn't help but feel lucky because despite how poor my parents were, they had never given me up to anyone.

Young monks walked past us, but *mae* didn't ask one to stop. I asked her why she didn't. She said, 'Pumpkin, we need to find the humblest and holiest one in order to make the most merit out of our offerings.'

She was right. The higher the being you make your offering to, the more merit you make. For example, you can make more merit from feeding one person than from feeding ten animals because a human is a higher being.

'Now help *mae* look for a sedate monk with bare feet and no *dek wat*,' she said.

Serendipitously, a bald, middle-aged monk wrapped in a saffron robe appeared. My mother called, '*Nimon jao ka*,' a formal greeting reserved only for monks. You have to call a monk to stop, or else he will walk on because no monk can stop to ask for offerings. It is immodest. He can accept only voluntary offerings.

We sat before him on our knees to show appropriate respect, as in Buddhism, men are considered higher beings than women. We gently placed food and a lotus flower into his bowl, and as we *wai*'d, he blessed us.

I made an offering to the monk in order to get my wish. It is the Buddhist way; you must do something good to have something good done to you in return. I went off to school, hoping and praying that I had made the list. And I had. I raced home after school to tell my parents. This is a particularly fond memory for me, as it is the one time when I felt that my parents were rooting for me and wanting something for me as much as I did.

I was thrilled with the meagre pass I had achieved—I came second-last in my class—and delightedly informed my father that I was very proud of myself. He smiled and told me that I had every reason to be. The exam hadn't been easy at all, and there had been fierce competition amongst the students.

That day stands out in my mind as the last time that I had a real interest in my education, and that I wanted something from it so badly.

The only thing I really liked about school was that I got to hang out with my best friends, Veena and Somsri. We played together during the lunch break, which was, unsurprisingly, my favourite part of the school day. I envied Veena for her intelligence; she received A's in all her assignments. Of course she got a lot of extra tutoring at home from her mother, who was a teacher. Somsri was more like me; poor and ignorant. The three of us got on very well and hardly ever argued.

It was certainly an innocent time for me, and our amusements were simple. Our favourite game was where we flicked tamarind seeds at each other.

During the twice-yearly school holidays, my brother, sister, and I were sent away separately to stay with our aunt and uncle on their farm in another province in Isan. We always enjoyed these visits, but I was a bit puzzled as to why we couldn't ever stay at home. It is obvious to me now that it was for economic reasons. My mother's gambling debts were increasing, and getting through a few months without having to feed us was a mercy on my parents' meagre finances.

Meanwhile, we were having the time of our lives and being spoilt rotten by our doting relatives. They delighted in surprising us with sweets and ice-cream, and could never refuse us. We also got to play and run riot with our numerous cousins, finding dung beetles, frogs, and grasshoppers, all of which would be deep-fried for dinner.

This arrangement seemed to be mutually beneficial for all the family. When we arrived home to the base, everyone seemed pleased enough to see one another.

I would have loved it if, just once, our parents could have come away with us too. There were plenty of places near my uncle's cassava farm where *por* and I could have fished together, and I'm sure my mother would have enjoyed gossiping and cooking with her sisters.

POVERTY SEVERELY LIMITS your choices. During the last semester of ninth grade the debates started about who would stay in school and who couldn't afford to. The bright kids from relatively financially stable backgrounds, including my friend Veena, were planning to attend a well-known school in Bangkok, while the rest of us, more than half of the class, knew that we were coming to the end of our school days. My older brother had also given up school in ninth grade because the government doesn't fund your education after this point.

I was completely indifferent, however, as school had long since bored me. My homework was constantly incomplete since I had gotten into the habit of just leaving the parts I couldn't do instead of asking for help. My contributions in class were at an all-time low because I felt marginalised by my lack of academic know-how. I must have given up on myself. I believed that I was good for nothing and, therefore, couldn't see the point in continuing the struggle to learn.

I was tired of getting up early to sit on the green army bus every morning and then arrive home to an empty house while *mae* was out gambling. And so, I left school without any qualms or interest at just 15 years of age—I have a lot of regrets in my life, but this remains my biggest one to date.

CHAPTER 2

As TIME PASSED, my mother's daily absences became longer and longer, often leaving my siblings and I to fend for ourselves.

There were times when we were forced to go to the gambling house to beg her for money to buy food; other times I would just plead with her to cook. *Mae*'s answer never varied—a wave of the hand and a casual promise to follow me home in a few minutes. If we persisted, she would tell us to go away by shouting '*pai pai!*' and raise her hand to scare us.

My pleas fell on deaf ears each time I asked for her help. She never took notice of us children because she was too wrapped up in her gambling compulsion, a habit as addictive as heroin.

My younger sister and I were the ones who suffered. My brother Nop had by this time moved to Bangkok in search of work, but also to escape the troubles that overwhelmed our lives.

We had never been that close; however, I did miss his affection. Nop had played mother to me, cooking *kai dao* (fried egg) for me when I was young, while *mae* spent her time gambling and drinking with her friends. I can still recall memories of him hanging mosquito nets over my bed. He was just a boy himself when he accepted responsibility for me. I cherish these memories as they are a rare reminder of an innocent time in my childhood.

What semblance of childhood I had vanished when my brother left. I began to lead a life with no structure to it. I would sit in front of a television screen watching soap operas all day. I did as I pleased. I didn't know what parental guidance was.

The soap opera *Dao Phra Suk*, which means Venus, became my staple diet. It told the story of a girl called Dao, who had been abandoned by her mother at the hospital immediately after her birth. She lived a miserable childhood. She was treated like a slave by her adoptive mother, who forced her to clean her house as if she were a poor servant girl. She eventually ran away from home, only to end up in a brothel where she remained until she was rescued by love.

I often compared my own plight to that of Dao. Although she suffered more than I, her dignity and morale remained firmly intact. She was a true survivor. When she worked as a prostitute, she deceived men into thinking that they had slept with her by plying them with liquor until they were rendered senseless.

I often wished I had her strength. I secretly prayed to Buddha, asking him to bless Dao so she could find love and escape the demons that haunted her. When I prayed for Dao's happiness, though, I was actually praying for my own. I didn't know what true happiness was, but I knew that poverty had no role to play in it.

MY LIFE WAS turned upside down the year I turned 17. That was the year in which my parents separated.

Although I had always suspected it to be inevitable, I was still devastated by their break up. *Mae's* addiction to gambling had become exhausting and knew no bounds. As in most of these incidents, I cannot remember exactly when it happened, but I recall that she vanished for three days. She had gone to a friend's house and gambled what little money she had in her possession. I had always been charged with the unenviable task of taking her home every night when she got drunk and could no longer find the way.

For my mother, gambling was a means of escape. For me, her addiction was a source of embarrassment. I hated her for it. I resented having to call to the 'gambling house' every few hours, where I was always made to feel unwelcome by *mae's* friends for obvious reasons.

Por, on the other hand, had never been one to lose face. Thai men will tolerate all sorts of behaviour rather than risk a confrontation. Fetching your gambling-addicted wife is out of the question and emasculating. But on that day, *por* had had enough and took matters into his own hands. This was most unlike him because it is not the Thai way.

When he discovered *mae* had been gone for three days, he was more than prepared to lose face. And I, for one, wasn't going to miss it.

The house where *mae* was staying was a short walk from ours. *Por* made the journey in less than two minutes and thumped on the front door. When no one answered, he opened it and called to my mother from the doorway, 'You come home right now or I will find myself another *mia*. I am serious this time.'

I was standing less than six feet behind him. Although I had seen my parents argue before, I had never seen *por* lose his temper like this.

The women inside remained silent, and *por* stood as still as a statue while my mother taunted him: 'Well if you can get yourself another wife you better do so because I'm not coming home yet.'

He made no reply but closed the door to an outburst of laughter. This was perhaps the greatest insult that *mae* could have delivered.

I turned and walked away. I didn't want him to know that I had witnessed this, though I think by that stage he no longer cared enough to be embarrassed.

I ran home, sat in front of the television, and pretended to be oblivious to the events that had just taken place. As it transpired, I need not have worried because he didn't come home after the incident.

I fell asleep at some stage, only to be woken by the sound of someone howling.

It was *mae*. I crept downstairs and saw her standing in the middle of the room, screaming and waving a broom. Her outbursts of anger were nothing new to me. What was new was the other woman standing beside my father, holding a suitcase.

I recognised her. She worked as a 'singer' in a nightclub which my father frequented.

You *farang*s might not understand what these 'singers' do. In my culture, such labels are given to conceal the true nature of such a woman's work. These women entertain men by offering them a mixture of song, sexual favours, and conversation. They engage in long-term relationships with men and like to be showered with presents and money in return for their attentions.

I was immediately struck by her presence, not simply because she was there, but because she was unmoved by my mother's distress and rage.

She ignored her threats and, instead, calmly surveyed our house.

My father stood firm beside her. His eyes were void of any emotion. *Mae* had gone too far this time. In truth, I knew this moment signalled the end of my family as I knew it. I had been through some hard times because of *mae*, but I didn't like her replacement at all.

I had seen this woman before in a photograph my father had taken. I had disliked her immediately, though I recognised what my father saw in her. In Thailand, we say that an old ox likes fresh grass. This woman was alluring and younger than *mae*, who had unfortunately not weathered life too well.

Although my father wasn't a rich man, this woman knew she was approaching an age when she would no longer be able to work—time waits for no woman.

So she fell in love with *por*. I suspect that he loved her in return and had confided in her, making him more vulnerable to seduction.

Such relationships are normal in Thailand. It is called surviving, and the fact that *por* had a wife and three children was not relevant. I think she thought we could all live together. You might consider this an outrageous proposition, but polygamy is not a strange concept in Thailand. Although it is illegal, it is still very common and accepted. Wealthy men often maintain more than one *mia*, and each one is categorised. The official wife, the *mia luang*, usually comes from another family of equal standing. She would be permitted to accompany the man to social events.

The second wife is called a *mia noi* and is chosen by the man. In past times, the third wife was usually a slave whose parents sold her to the groom. She would do the chores, but she could also be called upon to produce children. In my culture, the number of wives a man possesses is a reflection of his wealth and virility.

As I sat there watching my parents' marriage fall apart, I couldn't help but wonder if *mae* would accept this woman into our home.

My only experience of such situations was gained from watching soap operas where the first wife was usually depicted as evil, though occasionally she could be tolerant.

Mae was neither tolerant nor generous, which became ever clearer during this confrontation.

There was no reasoning with her. She screamed, shouted, and issued insult after insult. She raised the broom and repeatedly attempted to hit *por* and his mistress on the head, then tried to sweep them out the door.

While my mother screamed obscenities and issued undignified threats, *por*'s lover continued to ignore her as if it was beneath her dignity to react in any way.

She never even squinted her eyes. If I had been an objective witness, I might have admired the dignified stance she adopted in the face of *mae*'s rage.

Por also remained calm and showed no visible reaction. In fact, neither he nor his lover spoke; they just waited for my mother to tire herself out.

I now believe *por* had contemplated introducing a *mia noi* to *mae* for some time. I think he may have convinced himself that *mae* would be indifferent to such a proposal since she no longer loved him or cared for him. Thai women tend to be pragmatic and in such cases usually share their husband.

Having shouted at and threatened *por*, *mae* issued an ultimatum.

'I don't want this bitch in my house. If you want that *garee* (whore), I'll take the kids, and you will never see them or me again!'

If it had been within my power, I would have forced the woman to leave myself.

My memory of the events of that night is, even today, as clear as if they happened yesterday. I can recall looking at *por* and silently beseeching him to rid our home of his consort, but he never said a word. I think *mae* knew he had already made his choice.

I looked on in silence as his *mia noi* stood there, waiting for *mae* to leave.

Mae left home that night to stay with a relative, leaving my sister and me behind. As much as I wanted to, I neither slept nor cried that night.

Though *mae* had abandoned us, she was still my family. I felt hurt that *por* could choose a prostitute above *mae*, my sister, and me. It made no sense to me no matter what way I tried to rationalise the situation. I didn't yet know the impact his decision would have on my life.

Moments later, my father sat my sister and me down to discuss our future. His words sounded almost sinister. He told us that we could live with him and his new wife, whom he asked us to call *naa*, which means aunt. But he must have known this would never happen.

He spoke in a calm and measured tone and asked us not to be angry with him, that he loved *naa*, and that she was a kind woman. We listened to him in disbelief.

THE NEXT MORNING, *mae* returned home and woke us from our sleep.

She calmly explained that we had to pack our belongings because we were leaving for Bangkok, which Thais call Krung Thep, the City of Angels, later that morning.

I was stunned. Two nights previous, life was as it had always been. Now my family had divided, and another woman had become *por's mia noi*.

I began packing what few possessions I had. While I resented *mae* for taking me away from home, I knew *naa* would never have allowed me to live there. It was her home now.

I had always doubted my mother's ability to look after herself, and I had even less confidence in her ability to look after my sister and me, but she suddenly seemed very organised and business-like. She focused on what she needed to do to overcome what had happened. I had never seen this side of her personality before.

As YOU MIGHT have expected, news of the disintegration of my parents' marriage spread fast in the army base.

Local women began arriving at our home to offer their condolences and to glare accusingly at my father. But he was beyond caring what anyone thought at this point.

Mae remained calm and accepted the little trinkets offered to her. I now know the experience was utterly humiliating for her, and she privately said that many of those who visited believed she had got what she deserved.

Mae also knew that her actions had contributed to the breakdown of her marriage, along with my father's philandering.

I was already surprised at the change of character I perceived in *mae*, but I was soon to discover how little I really knew her. When she thought no one was listening, one of her relatives mentioned that she had recently spoken with *mae*'s ex-husband.

Ex-husband! I was forced to place my hand over my mouth to prevent myself from screaming the news out loud.

I could not understand how *mae* could have kept an ex-husband a secret for so long. I would later learn that she had once been married to a Chinese man. It was a brief relationship because of his infidelity. I could not help but pity her for finding herself caught again in the same situation.

I asked myself question after question. Had she married her first husband for love and settled into a form of complacency that drove him into the arms of someone else?

It is difficult to imagine how she must have felt all those years ago. But I do believe that *mae* had expected *por* to continue financing her gambling addiction while she did nothing to address her insurmountable problems. You must remember that counselling had yet to be invented.

What I remember most about that morning was *por*'s body language.

As I walked out the door for the last time, I turned to *por* and said, 'Don't worry. I'll come and visit you often.'

Por smiled. On the inside, I believe his heart was breaking, though he dared not show any emotion for fear of losing face.

Mae left without saying a word, not even a goodbye to my father. She didn't even look back to gauge his reaction.

Por also remained expressionless. 'That's alright, dear, just be good to your mother and don't give her any trouble.' We didn't hug or kiss goodbye. That is not the Thai way.

Mae, my sister, and I went to the nearest bus terminal in Khorat where *mae* bought three bus tickets to Bangkok.

It was a surreal journey. My parents were now two separate entities, instead of just one.

My home, which I'd had no interest in leaving, was now a thing of the past. I feared the city. I knew I was embarking on a journey to an unknown place, where my childhood would soon be forgotten. The next part of my life was about to begin.

CHAPTER 3

THE BUS JOURNEY to Bangkok was not the sepia-toned family holiday that I had dreamed of as a young girl. *Mae* was inconsolable; it would be many years later before she would fully come to terms with the reality of what had happened.

I sat in the seat behind my mother and sister so that I could gaze out at the passing countryside and have some time to myself to think. *Mae*, on the other hand, talked incessantly in an obvious bid to enlist our sympathy and support. She blamed *por* for everything and, of course, took no responsibility for her own actions. I decided against pointing out the obvious because it would have been a futile exercise.

I wanted to ask her exactly how much money she had, but decided against it, knowing that I would be disappointed with the answer. I had no choice but to trust that she had some sort of plan.

The heavy bags under *mae*'s eyes revealed how tired she was, and I couldn't help but feel a little sorry for her. I smiled at her purposefully anytime she turned around to look at me; the daughter trying to reassure the mother that everything would be okay.

I was equally exhausted as I had barely slept the previous night. After *mae* had fled the house, *por* had decided to become intimate with his *mia noi*. And I had unfortunately been privy to every whispered word, every movement of the bed, and the constant pleas to my father to 'do it'.

I drifted in and out of sleep several times during the bus journey.

About an hour before we reached Bangkok, *mae* announced to my sister and me her grand plan to go into business. We listened in stunned silence. This newly confident and capable woman outlined how she planned to purchase a vending cart from which she would sell home-cooked papaya salad.

My initial scepticism disappeared as I realised that it wasn't such a bad idea. *Mae* also decided that my sister should continue on with her education. I was both surprised and relieved by this decision. Finishing school would give my sister the opportunity to really make something of her life.

At that moment, I understood why I had been allowed to leave school early. My parents had believed that educating a girl like me was about as useful as playing the fiddle to a buffalo. This realisation was to the forefront of my mind as the bus pulled into the station, the old Moh Chit in the Jatujak district of Bangkok.

Bangkok, the City of Angels, mesmerised me. I had never before seen so much traffic, and I found myself longing to return to the wide-open spaces of Khorat. Bangkok reminded me of a disturbed ant hill; it was teeming with people who were frantically rushing in all directions, trying to reach some unknown goal.

As we stepped off the bus and into this alien world, I was immediately struck by the differences between the local people and my mother, sister and me. Their clothes were more modern and they carried all sorts of gadgets with them, many of which I had never even seen before. Most of the locals were in too much of a hurry to pay us any attention, but to the ones who did glance in our direction, we must have looked like country bumpkins on our first visit to the big city.

Would I ever be able to settle here? I asked myself.

Then my thoughts turned to *por*. I wished he was here to protect us. A wave of sadness washed over me as I realised that such a reunion was unlikely and that this strange and busy city was to be my new home whether I liked it or not.

I turned to look for *mae* and saw her walking away from me.

'Wait there, Pumpkin,' she called, 'I'll just be a few minutes.'

I was happy to people-watch, but my sister Nang was restless. She told me that she needed to use the toilet, but I had heard horror stories of gangs preying on innocent girls like us, so I refused to let her out of my sight.

'When *mae* comes back, I'll take you to the toilet. I need to go too.'

'And I'm also hungry.'

'Yes, well so am I. Look, I'm sure *mae* has money for food. Just be patient. *Por* told me that we were to be good and not cause any problems. Okay?'

'Hmphh! We're not to cause any problems, but it's alright for him to upset her, and us too.'

All of a sudden her eyes welled up, and she turned and hid her face from me. I gave her a hug and whispered that everything would be okay. She wiped her tears away, ashamed of being emotional in public.

'Pumpkins,' *mae* called out.

We gathered our possessions and made our way towards *mae*, who was now smiling broadly.

'I've good news and bad news. Which would you like first?'

Without waiting for a reply, she continued, 'The good news is that I've managed to talk to my friend Pa, and we're going to see her this evening. The bad news is we've to get on another bus.'

She pulled a funny face, making us laugh and temporarily forget about the second bus journey that awaited us.

'Are you hungry? Let's go find the bathroom and then get some dinner.'

As we walked, *mae* explained that Pa used to live near the camp with her husband and three children. She had left her husband after he beat her up once too often. *Mae* said he had been a heavy drinker who regularly accused his wife of having affairs.

As we walked, I was assaulted by a deluge of new scents, sights, and sounds. The numerous cars never stopped honking their horns, and their fumes made the hot air pungent. My eyes were doing cartwheels in my head trying to take it all in.

We ate pork skewers and beef from a market stall located outside the station. *Mae* continued to talk, explaining that Pa lived in a district called Bang Na, a suburb of Bangkok.

The food quietened our growling stomachs and served as a temporary distraction to our problems. I guessed that this visit to Pa was not merely social and that she must have offered to let us stay with her.

Although it would take two hours to travel there, at least we had somewhere to go, somewhere to leave our bags, and somewhere to call our own. I was sure this had to be a good omen for the future.

Even after all these years, it is hard for me to describe, let alone comprehend, *mae*'s feelings about what had happened. But at that moment in time, she appeared to be more concerned with stepping forward into the future rather than drowning in the quicksand of the past.

THE JOURNEY TO Pa's home was more tiring than the first trip, although it was a shorter journey. There was no air-conditioning on the bus and the heat was stifling. At times, the smell of petrol fumes overwhelmed me. I tried to take my mind off the conditions on the bus by concentrating on the sights of the city.

I had never seen skyscrapers, or the three-wheeled *tuk-tuk*s, or such large numbers of *farang*s in any one place.

The noise also perturbed, and at times, deafened me. I felt threatened by this new world and wondered if we were well enough equipped to survive here.

On the bus, *mae* began to discuss her troubles with a strange woman seated next to her.

Such casual conversations may be considered normal in Western society, but it is not so in Thailand. *Mae* spoke openly about *por*'s 'whore' and recounted the story of how she had defended her honour with a sweeping brush. Of course, she failed to mention her own gambling addiction.

The woman listened attentively and occasionally laughed out loud. She mentioned that her eldest daughter had recently chased a prospective *mia* from her kitchen, causing her husband to fall to his knees and beg her for forgiveness.

From the moment they began talking, *mae*'s voice grew louder and more animated. I closed my eyes and hoped that she would fall silent, but this, to my shame, did not happen. By the time we reached our stop, our fellow passengers knew the most intimate details of my parents' marriage.

Our destination was Bang Na, a small town surrounded by fields and trees. The setting immediately relaxed me, as it reminded me of home.

Pa was waiting at the bus stop with her three children when we arrived. She looked genuinely delighted to see us.

Her children smiled shyly at me. Grateful for their warmth, I eagerly returned their smiles.

My exhaustion must have been etched all over my face because Pa patted me on the back and said, 'Don't worry, it isn't far.'

Mae recounted the events of the previous evening to Pa as we walked. I heard my father's name mentioned once or twice, and slowed my pace to avoid the inevitable mention of the word whore.

Pa's youngest son walked alongside me. He was too shy to talk until I asked him where his friends lived and if he liked to play football. My questions prompted an outpouring of conversation. He described his school, his classroom, his teacher, and so forth.

We reached our new home minutes later. Pa had warned us that our room was empty, but said she knew where we could buy cheap furniture.

We were just so happy to have a roof over our heads that we didn't mind the bareness.

From the moment we met her, Pa made us feel welcome. Once we had settled in, she brought us upstairs to her flat, where she offered us soft drinks. As she poured the drinks, she apologised for not being able to do more for us. She spoke of the difficulties she had faced when she first arrived in Bang Na. Her story was one of endurance in the face of adversity. Listening to her gave us hope for our own situation, and it lightened the atmosphere considerably that evening. *Mae* certainly appreciated her efforts because she declared, without a hint of irony, that Pa had done more for us than my father ever did. Pa looked slightly embarrassed by this comment, but she soon regained her composure, and went to fetch us some blankets to sleep on. She also gave us some cleaning materials, telling us that she had scrubbed her own flat clean on the night she moved in. '*Mai pen rai*,' she said every time we thanked her. 'Don't mention it'.

OUR ROOM WAS located on the ground floor and we had a miniature backyard in which to dry our clothes. The small room that was to be our new home didn't look too welcoming, but *mae* assured us that with a few pieces of furniture, it could be made more homely.

I, for one, had not been able to understand how *mae* had been able to afford the move to Bangkok. This mystery was solved when she confessed that she had borrowed a few thousand baht from a relative in Khorat and had left the responsibility of clearing the debt with my father.

I nodded my head in agreement when she told me that she'd had no alternative, though I suspected her original intent was to spend the money gambling.

We slept soundly that first night.

Pa brought *mae* out early the next morning to help her pursue her street-vending plan. When she returned that evening, she was the proud owner of a cart and cooking equipment.

The prospect of running her own business had ignited a fervour in my mother that neither my sister nor I had ever witnessed before. *Mae* had even walked around the industrial area in search of the optimum location for her stall. She finally settled on a spot that was both close to our building and also convenient to the nearby factories.

I was astonished by my mother's newly developed business sense. Her plan, contrary to my expectations, seemed to be well thought-out.

She discussed the venture in great detail with me. She hoped to purchase some chairs and foldaway tables for her customers, adding that her food would be cheap but delicious.

As for my role in the venture, I was free to find another job if I wanted. But for the first time in my life the prospect of spending time with my mother actually appealed to me. It was becomingly increasingly clear to me that I didn't really know her at all and I saw the job as an opportunity to change this. I also thought that it would be a nice and safe way of getting to know Bang Na.

The work on the stall turned out to be unrelenting. It being my first job, I found it difficult to rise early and spend the entire day standing on my feet. The work itself was also very demanding. Every morning at 5am, *mae* would wake up and go to the market near Bang Na junction to buy ingredients. She also took care of the cooking and, once again, contrary to my expectations, she was very good at it.

Customer care was my responsibility, as I was 'chief server', though I also helped prepare the vegetables, playing kitchen hand to *mae*. We weren't an idyllic team as everything was so new to us and we were both struggling to learn the ropes.

Not surprisingly, considering my later profession, I discovered that I liked dealing with people once I overcame my initial nervousness. But *mae* was always more outgoing than I and she became very friendly with some of the more frequent customers.

There were quite a few people from Khorat, and many others from provinces in northeastern Thailand, living in Bang Na. Like us, they had come to Bangkok in search of work. Many became regulars at our stall, not because we came from Khorat, but because the food we served was delicious.

Mae would spend hours preparing mortar after mortar of *som tam*, a spicy papaya salad from Laos and the Isan region of Thailand. *Som* means 'sour' in Isan and Lao, and *tam* translates as 'pounded'.

The main ingredient for this dish was grated papaya, which *mae* pounded with a pestle and mortar. She usually added chilli, garlic, lime, dried shrimp, peanuts and fish sauce, depending on the customers' tastes.

Mae also cooked *larb*, a type of Thai and Lao meat salad, for which we charged 15 baht per serving.

Business was always good, but I found myself both loving and hating the work in equal measure. Though I liked dealing with the public, I eventually came to resent *mae*.

In between smiling at the customers, we would snipe and bitch at each other. She continuously moaned about the customers, whom I considered to be our saviours. They, after all, paid for my sister's education and the roof over our heads.

Mae had, until this time, run the business as best she could, but when she settled into city life, her old habits returned. To be fair, she wasn't as bad as she had been in Khorat. For one thing, her new friends all worked during the day, which ensured they could only gamble at the weekends. But more importantly, *mae* was more careful with money now that it was her own she was spending.

I BEGAN DREAMING about *por* every night. I found myself wondering how he was coping without us and whether he even missed my sister and me. I eventually decided to return home to visit him despite *mae*'s objections.

I was still hopeful that he might want us back if I could convince him of how much *mae* had changed for the better.

I travelled to Khorat by bus, alone this time. From the first moment I saw him, I sensed that *por* had settled into his new life. This became all the more apparent when I spoke to him of the improvements in *mae*'s behaviour. Rather than beg us to come home, he instead seemed to be personally insulted by these changes in my mother.

He remained quite bitter over the whole episode and was adamant that he never wanted to talk to her again. Although he looked good, and the stress was gone from his face, there was a sadness in his eyes that suggested how much he missed us.

I returned home dispirited. I had hoped for a reunion between my parents despite everything that had happened. Of course, I realised that this dream was to forever remain in the realm of fantasy.

The bonds holding the rest of my family together felt very tenuous, and I feared that we were in danger of complete collapse.

At my mother's request, I wrote a letter to my brother inviting him to come and see us. We hadn't seen him since he left Khorat. I was curious to see his reaction to the news that *por* had taken a second wife.

He turned up to have dinner with us some days later. When *mae* recounted the story to him, he was unmoved.

I knew that *mae*'s gambling and long absences had deeply affected him as a young boy, but she didn't seem to realise this. He could not hide his lack of emotion. The truth was that he had moved on with his life.

He promised he would visit and give us money whenever he could spare it, but I knew that he had emotionally detached himself from us long ago. He had made his own life in Bangkok, and we no longer featured in it.

CHAPTER 4

THE DISINTEGRATION OF my family had a profound effect on me. I missed *por*, and at times I couldn't help but wonder how different my life might have been if he and *mae* had remained married.

Although they had never provided a perfect home, they had at least created a semblance of normality. I now felt completely bereft. I feared that I was destined to spend the rest of my life working on a rickety food stall. My life seemed to stretch out before me like a long and never-ending road, with no real destination in sight.

Back then, I was what we Thais call a *baan nok*. It is a derogatory name that my people use to describe naïve country bumpkins. I do not pretend that the decisions I made were the correct ones. They were merely short-term solutions aimed at bringing about a change in my circumstances.

The first thing I decided to do was stop working for *mae* and to seek employment elsewhere.

Our relationship had become unbearable. She treated me with utter disrespect in front of our customers, frequently bossing me around and shouting at me. People came from far and wide to feast on my mother's mouth-watering dishes, but the side-helping of dirty laundry that came free of charge left a bitter aftertaste. I eventually lost count of the number of times my mother caused me to lose face.

When I had been humiliated one too many times, I found work in a nearby factory. Though I earned just 200 baht a day for this menial labour, the independence it afforded me was invaluable. Besides, there weren't many choices for women with my level of education.

I gradually began to realise that rather than moving towards any particular goal, I was simply standing still. This realisation sent me into a downward spiral of depression.

Mae's contributions towards my lack of self-esteem and anxiety were considerable. Not only was I not worthy of education but I was also to blame for not attracting potential husbands. In Thailand, women of my standing are expected by their families to marry anyone willing to take them as a bride; being selective is a luxury we cannot afford.

I had never felt attracted to men. I thought of them as curious creatures, almost like the strange turtles and frogs that swam in the ponds.

Mae had become fixated on this particular aspect of my life and took it upon herself to play the role of matchmaker. She committed herself to the pursuit of the ideal suitor in the belief that this was what was best for me.

The man she eventually settled on was called Chai. He was reasonably attractive and about ten years older than me. He had moved into our building in Bang Na and introduced himself to *mae* when he heard our family came from Khorat, as he had grown up there.

Mae considered Chai a true gentleman in the Thai sense because he approached the bride-to-be through her mother. She often commented on his impeccable manners, stylish dress sense, intelligent conversation and Indian-like features.

At first, I paid very little attention to her infatuation with him as I didn't understand her motivation in forming a relationship with a younger man. It was only as time passed that her real intentions became clear. And Chai, to my surprise, proved to be a willing accomplice.

With *mae*'s approval, he took advantage of every opportunity to engage me in conversation. He reminisced about his childhood, and talked about the different people we were both acquainted with in Khorat. But despite his best efforts, my interest in all conversations with him invariably waned.

He told me that he had been raised by his aunt following the death of his parents, and that he was now working as a bartender. I then discovered exactly what it was about him that had my mother so enthralled: he had inherited his aunt's house in Khorat when she died. His wealth was of no interest to me, however, and I likened him to a giant-sized mosquito that refused to be swatted away. Our relationship, if you could call it that, was an unfortunate one.

Chai was the only man I knew who spoke about politics and regularly read broadsheet newspapers. A bumpkin like me knew nothing of such things, but I would smile politely and look suitably impressed when he spoke about modern society's ills and other serious matters.

I tried to find the courage to tell my mother that I had no interest in Chai, but in Thailand, the financial standing of a man is considered more important than anything else when it comes to marriage. The stability of a relationship is decided on a financial rather than an emotional basis, rendering love irrelevant. The fact that Chai would be able to support *mae* and me made him the perfect partner in her eyes.

Chai persevered in his efforts to capture my attention, though at times it appeared to me that he attracted no one's attention but *mae*'s.

When he did eventually muster up the courage to ask me to watch a film, *mae* almost danced with joy. I was foolish enough to agree to the proposition, and so we went on a few dates. He showered me with presents, like my favourite teen magazine, *Thur Gab Chan* (You and Me), as well as candy and flowers. Gifts had been such a rarity in my life up until then that the receipt of so many all at once left me dizzy with exhilaration.

Although I was not sexually attracted to him, I came to like him because he treated me well.

I cannot help but smile when I think back to those early days of courtship. How naïve I was! The only knowledge I had of life and relationships was gleaned from soap operas and my own parents' disastrous marriage. Compared to these tumultuous relationships, what Chai and I shared appeared healthier than it actually was. So as time passed, I began to reconsider Chai's suitability as a potential husband.

During my few casual conversations with *mae* about Chai, his fondness for alcohol repeatedly raised its head. I had never known a man who did not become aggressive after consuming alcohol, or what we call *naam plian nisai*, 'habit-changing water', and Chai was no exception. I had seen him transform from his usual kind and gentle self into a sinister and aggressive man after the consumption of a few beers.

Such dramatic changes in personality weren't confined to the privacy of our own home. Once, when drinking in a local bar, he became very hostile towards the other customers. Convinced that everyone was staring at him, he began shouting, 'What the fuck are you looking at? What's your fucking problem? I'm drunk, do you have a problem with that?'

But no one in the bar took any notice of him. We Thais rarely take offence at drunken men because we recognise that they are not in their best mind.

Though Chai was my boyfriend, I was not in love with him. I was raised to believe that girls of my standing in society shouldn't waste their time daydreaming about romance. I was taught to be pragmatic. Besides, it wasn't like I had several suitors all vying for my affection, and I also had my mother's wishes to consider.

So three months after we first met, Chai asked me to move in with him, and I told him to seek my mother's blessing, assuming that this step was nothing more than a formality.

Chai spoke to *mae* that very evening. But before giving him an answer, she came to me and asked if this was what I wanted. I immediately replied that it was, knowing that this was the only answer she wanted to hear.

Mae didn't comment on my decision. We both knew that, should Chai ask, there was really only one answer to be given. Chai could offer us the stability we both craved. And despite his fondness for alcohol, we were both under the impression that he was a good man.

Mae later offered me a rare nugget of advice that I have never forgotten. She said, 'I wish you more happiness than I ever had. Use my marriage as an example of what not to do as a wife. Don't follow in my footsteps. Couples should work at understanding each other, and learn, and—more importantly—accept their partner's flaws. Nobody is perfect.'

Mae had never spoken so candidly to me before. It made me realise just how important my union with Chai was to her, as she stood to recoup the financial support she had lost when my father left her.

As we sat alone in the tiny room that had become our home, she admitted to all the mistakes she had made in the past. She conceded that she had treated my father badly. She also spoke openly about her love for gambling and finally admitted that this love had long since turned into an addiction. We stayed up talking into the early hours of the morning.

I realised that I had never really known *mae*. I knew the gambling addict, the disciplinarian, and the drunk; but I did not know the person that lay buried beneath these superficial outer layers.

My wedding was a small affair, hastily organised and held in the one room my family inhabited. Only a handful of friends attended because we could not afford to entertain many guests.

Our ceremony was a *koh ka ma*, which is one that is organised for situations when the bride-to-be is pregnant. The *koh ka ma* is the groom's way of asking his bride's parents to forgive him for his transgression. But I was not pregnant— we just couldn't afford a traditional wedding.

There was no chanting, music, monk, or Buddha involved. The only luxury I could afford was a white, embroidered dress. Chai wore a pair of jeans and a t-shirt. My pessimism on the day was intense.

Chai did not have the resources to pay a dowry for my hand. *Mae* was unperturbed by this, but I was both surprised and disappointed. Instead, Chai presented *mae* with a tray of lotus flowers and *sai sin*, along with a few thousand baht. *Sai sin* is thread, usually white, which is tied around the two wrists. We use it to wish good health and fortune on a person or couple.

Mae tied the thread around our wrists and blessed us individually. She asked Chai to take good care of her daughter. Then I knelt in front of her and she blessed me, saying that she hoped we would stay together forever and give her many grandchildren.

After the blessing, we left for a traditional Isan restaurant where we ate a feast of papaya salad, grilled chicken, and the spicy delicacy *neu nam tok*, which is grilled tenderloin of beef.

After much wrestling with my conscience I had decided against inviting *por* to the wedding. I knew *mae* would have been furious and possibly even have objected to his participation. I told him about the event only after it had taken place.

On our wedding night, I moved into Chai's room. Prior to this we had only ever exchanged kisses on the cheek, but that night we shared our first proper kiss and I lost my virginity.

Thai girls rarely discussed such private matters as sex with their friends in those days, so I had no idea what to expect. We were taught to keep ourselves for our husbands only, unlike men who would be praised by their peers for promiscuous behaviour. In fact, for some Thai men it is a rite of passage to lose their virginity with a prostitute.

When Chai lay down on the bed, I began trembling with nervousness and excitement, hoping that I could please him, though I was completely clueless as to how exactly I should go about this.

Recognising that I was nervous and inexperienced, Chai was quite gentle with me. He turned off the lights, and I instantly felt more relaxed about getting naked, and also about seeing a man's naked body for the first time.

Chai laid me down on the bed and caressed my body, eagerly fondling my breasts and kissing me passionately. As the naïve pupil, very little was required of me but to offer my body to him.

The consummation of our marriage didn't hurt too much or take too long. It was a lot more abrupt than I had expected. I had also envisioned Chai and me basking in a post-coital glow, talking about the day's events and about our future life together, as we lay nestled in each other's arms. Instead, when it was all over Chai had turned his back to me and fallen asleep immediately. It wasn't until much later in our marriage that I experienced my first orgasm.

I found sleeping with Chai almost impossible. He snored so loudly the bed trembled beneath us, and his every movement pierced my dreams and sent me tumbling back to reality.

Our life settled into a routine of sorts. We both went out to work each morning and returned home exhausted. Our sex life also became routine. We slept together about five times during our first few weeks of marriage. Chai had a very low sex drive, and I rarely succeeded in inciting any passion in him. He seemed to want me only once a week, which I thought strange for a young, healthy man.

As his wife, I never denied him, no matter how low my own level of desire might be. He was no fantasy lover, but he always tried to make lovemaking enjoyable for me. Unfortunately, he never really succeeded. To put it more crudely, he never turned me on.

A MONTH INTO my marriage I discovered I was pregnant. It was only after I fainted one morning and spent subsequent mornings staring down a toilet bowl that I decided to make an appointment to see a doctor. I knew nothing of these matters and although I had made several offerings for a child to the four-faced Brahma at Erawan Shrine, I was still surprised when the doctor announced that I was pregnant. Chai was overjoyed; he spent the next few days smiling so broadly I feared his face might crack.

The only cravings I experienced during my pregnancy were for sour fruit like *mayom* and raw mango, which I consumed in quantities that would have satisfied an elephant. *Mae* warned against eating spicy foods, which I had a particular weakness for, lest they burn my unborn baby's tongue.

In many ways, Chai became an exemplary husband. The impending arrival of our baby made him much more attentive, and he would often do the shopping and cleaning. He also took care of the laundry. He arranged our affairs with military-like precision. My only responsibility was to relax in preparation for the birth, and the days drifted slowly by in a haze of TV programmes.

In the beginning, the pregnancy had marked a turning point in our relationship. It had injected a new sense of purpose into our union.

However, about three months before I was due to give birth, I returned to our flat one evening to find Chai waiting for me. He was holding a letter that had been addressed to me by my doctor. I was immediately anxious and searched Chai's face for some emotion that would reveal the nature of the letter. But he was a blank canvas. I took the letter from him and read it; it was a request from my doctor that I visit his surgery, as an irregularity had been found in my blood test.

My first thought was for my unborn child and the possibility that he or she might be in danger. Feeling weak, I sat down. I was so deep in thought that I had forgotten all about Chai and had failed to notice his chilling silence. He stood motionless, arms folded, and with his eyes fixed on me.

Suddenly he began shouting, 'What the hell is going on? Did you fuck around on me? If you gave me anything . . . !'

He then raised his hand and struck me hard across the face, all the while screaming manically that he was going to kill me.

I reached my hand up to my face and could feel my cheek beginning to swell. I remember wondering distractedly if my cheek might in fact swell into a hand-shaped mound, complete with five distinct fingers.

I had never seen a man so angry that he turned the colour of a red chilli. I was about to plead with him to calm down when he punched me again with a clenched fist, this time making contact with the side of my head. For a second everything went black, and then colours slowly began to reappear in nondescript shapes. Despite my confusion, my first instinct was to protect my baby and so I placed one hand over my stomach and I held the other out blindly in front of me in a vain attempt to stop Chai should he charge at me again.

My vision gradually returned to normal and I saw Chai standing over me, his eyes still seething with rage. I begged him to calm down and call the doctor to see what was wrong with me before making such wild accusations, but he was beyond all reasoning. I struggled to my feet, prompting him to begin circling me, like a tiger stalking a deer. He then kicked me in the back, sending a horrific tremor of pain along my spine. The blood-curdling scream this elicited seemed to jolt him back to his senses. I didn't utter another sound for fear of provoking a second attack.

I was aware that he had grown increasingly possessive during our marriage. He had made no secret of how much he hated me talking to other men, even though the extent of these conversations was usually just a polite 'hello'.

But I had never imagined that he would go so far as to physically attack me.

When he finally stopped shouting at me, I scrambled to my feet. All of a sudden Chai's anger turned to regret and he started showering me with apologies and excuses for his overreaction. A tense silence followed—even if I'd been able to find the words to reply to him, I doubt that I'd have managed to locate my voice beneath all the layers of shock and pain his attack had caused me.

The next morning, he accompanied me to the doctor. We were informed that the check-up was just precautionary and that I had nothing to worry about. Like the flick of a light switch, Chai reverted back to normal, and it was as though the previous evening had never happened.

That evening was to mark a turning point in our marriage, and it wasn't long before Chai's darker side resurfaced. His behaviour deteriorated rapidly, and over the next few weeks it was marked by an increasing fondness for alcohol. He started drinking with his colleagues after work. He would subsequently arrive home to me in the early hours of the morning in a state of complete intoxication. In such drunken stupors, he would adopt the role of the pitiful husband and mumble about what a disloyal wife I was and how he had been duped into an unrequited love.

'Why don't you love me? I loved you the moment I laid eyes on you in Khorat, but you never noticed me, did you?'

When he got really drunk, so drunk that he couldn't talk without slurring his words, he would proclaim without irony, 'You don't love me now, do you? You don't care about me at all!'

I varied my reactions in an effort to find the right one, but always in vain. Sometimes silence was the only way to get him to go to sleep, and other times it would result in an attack.

The next morning, like clockwork, he would be full of apologies and false promises.

I didn't seek advice from *mae* because I did not want to lose face. Instead, I tried to convince myself that his relationship with alcohol was more of a flirtation than a full-blown affair. His descent into addiction was gradual at first, but it soon began to gather pace.

When I reached the later stages of my pregnancy and was close to giving birth, Chai finally succumbed to the full power of addiction. He drank most nights and would stagger home drunk and disorientated.

Whether he was drunk or sober, I was too terrified to argue with him and I knew that any criticism of his behaviour would fall on deaf ears or, even worse, provoke an attack that would injure our unborn baby.

Why didn't I seek help? The truth is that I simply didn't know how to handle the situation. It broke my heart to watch Chai lose himself to drink. But one of the hardest things to bear during this time, aside from the physical abuse, was the fact that a lot of Chai's drunken accusations were, in fact, true. I had never loved him. I had only agreed to marry him for the same reason many Thai women marry their husbands—because I wanted companionship and someone who could provide for me and my family.

Ironically, as our relationship and marriage fell apart, our financial circumstances began to improve. Chai managed to restrict his drinking to outside of working hours and so he continued to earn a good salary. In time we were able to move into a bigger room. I had hoped that the move would offer us a fresh start and that we could confine what had happened to the realms of history, but this proved to be nothing more than wishful thinking. Three days after the move, Chai beat me once more. As with a lot of the beatings, I can no longer recall what prompted the attack. What I do remember, with crystal clarity, is each individual blow he dealt me.

The prospect of putting up with this violence for the rest of my life was unthinkable, and yet I felt anaesthetised by fear. So I suffered on in silence as my stomach continued to grow.

For the last month of the pregnancy I moved in with *mae*. I worried that if I stayed with Chai, my waters might break when he was on yet another drinking binge, and I would have no one to bring me to the hospital. My mother was oblivious to the beatings and mental torture Chai was subjecting me to, but she was aware of how much he drank and so she was equally concerned that I might be alone when the baby came.

As it turned out, both my mother and Chai were by my side for the birth in Rajvithi Hospital. After three hours of excruciating contractions, my son entered this world. When the nurse handed him over to me, I gazed at him in astonishment. He was so tiny and fragile. Up to that point in time I had never truly grasped the concept of unconditional love, but it now lay wrapped in a blanket in my arms, personified in my perfect baby boy, Geng. I think that on some level my baby sensed what I'd had to go through to bring him into this world, and that strengthened our bond even further.

Chai's impersonation of a doting father was flawless, but we both knew the truth. Again, I hoped and prayed that he would change and that our relationship would improve. I even tried to convince myself that the birth of our son would transform Chai, but I was only deluding myself. At first his behaviour did improve, and he even stopped drinking, but within weeks, he was back to his old ways, beating me and accusing me of sleeping with other men.

The problem I faced at the time was how to protect my son and leave Chai, without losing face. But I eventually realised that my son's welfare was more important than losing face. I decided to return to my father's home in Khorat, taking Geng with me.

Chai didn't follow, which surprised me a little, though I suspected he was too ashamed to face my father under the circumstances.

The sight of me returning home with a baby in tow and no father in sight sent the neighbourhood into a tailspin of gossip, but *por*'s warm greeting had the effect of muting their whispers.

Though we had not seen each other in over a year, the bond that existed between us was as strong as ever and *por* knew instantly that something was wrong. I poured my heart out to him, confessing every last detail, from the accusations of infidelity to the violent drunken attacks.

When I was finished, rather than tell me what to do, *por* told me that I must make my own decisions. I knew from his tone of voice that he would stand by me whatever I decided to do. He then astonished me by offering to raise my baby for me. The offer, although appreciated, was one that I couldn't possibly take him up on. I suspected that his new wife would not welcome my baby into her home.

Three days later, my mother joined us in Khorat. As with *por*, I told her everything. Although she knew Chai drank a lot, she had never suspected him of being violent and she looked positively crushed by my revelation. I think she also felt an element of guilt because she had been the driving force behind our marriage. She continued to stare at me for a long time afterwards, as if willing me to retract my confession and replace it with a fairy-tale version of my family life with Chai and our son.

My parents may not have given me a wonderful childhood, but they had never once raised a hand to me. When the reality of the situation with Chai had fully sunk in, both *por* and *mae* advised me to leave him. I had already devised a plan, which I outlined to my parents. I knew my mother still had a handful of relatives living in Khorat, so I suggested that she move back with my baby and take care of him until I could save up enough money to rent my own apartment. I had already spoken to my sister, and she had agreed to send as much money as she could to *mae* to help.

To my great surprise, *mae* agreed. In fact, she needed absolutely no convincing. She conceded that living in rural Thailand would be cheaper and it would also allow her to become closer to her grandson.

Once the decision was made, she rang Chai and brusquely informed him that she was looking after his son and that he was to send her money for his upkeep. Chai's pride was deeply wounded and he didn't argue with her.

I left the baby in *por*'s care until *mae* moved home. On my last day in Khorat, I met *por* and handed him a list of instructions, making him promise to contact me at the slightest sign of any problem. It broke my heart to leave my baby behind me, but I kept repeating over and over in my head that this was only a temporary arrangement and that before long I would be back for him. If I had known that I would never again live under the same roof as Geng, I may have reconsidered leaving him.

The return journey to Bangkok was a nightmare. My guilt and sorrow at leaving my child behind were so intense that they became like another passenger on the bus, refusing to budge from the seat beside me.

Back in Bangkok, I moved into a friend's apartment in the Ratchadapisek district. I missed the sense of independence and freedom that comes with having your own place, but then my home with Chai had come at a very high price.

I STARTED WORKING as a bartender in a bar on Surawong Road. I was glad of the distraction the job offered me but, unfortunately, Chai's workplace was located nearby.

When Chai heard that I was working there, he decided to pay me a visit, no doubt anticipating a dramatic and emotional reunion. But I was horrified to see him again and couldn't even bring myself to look him in the eye. The tension between us spread throughout the bar and the staff and customers alike looked on with baited breath to see how I would react. I finally found my voice, and in a cold, business-like tone, I asked him what he would like to drink, as though he were just another customer.

'Bua, can we talk?' he asked me in a low voice.

I responded curtly, telling him that I was too busy. His eyes widened in astonishment—

this was clearly not the reaction he had been expecting. Chai, aware of the multitude of heads turned in his direction, made a hasty retreat. I could hear him cursing the day I was born as he slammed the door behind him.

He returned the following day, carrying a bouquet of orchids. He clearly thought that a few smiles, false promises, and pretty flowers would be enough to entice me back.

'Please think about what our separation might do to our little boy,' he pleaded. 'Look at what happened with your parents. Please come back and we can try to be a family again. I'm a different person now. I love you.'

Deep down I knew that Chai hadn't changed and that his sweet words would eventually wither and die like the flower he had just given me. But my desire to be reunited with my baby coloured my judgement, and for a few moments I almost believed him. But just then Chai's gaze turned to my left, where my friend Somchai was seated, and his eyes glazed over in an instant.

'You are having an affair with that bastard, you bitch,' he shouted.

The bar fell deathly quiet. I could feel everyone's eyes boring holes in me as they awaited my response. All the beatings and mental torture I had suffered behind closed doors at the hands of Chai suddenly paled in comparison to his coming to my place of work and embarrassing me like this. I looked down at the bouquet I held in my hand. I closed my fingers over it and felt its beautiful, delicate petals crumple up. When I looked back up at Chai, the anger had vanished from his face and been replaced by a look of panic. In that instant, he knew it was over.

I didn't move from my seat, but quietly asked him to leave. He looked around, as if searching for someone to take his side, but the many pairs of eyes quickly turned the other way.

He slunk out of the bar, his shoulders hunched and his head bowed low, and I never saw him again.

CHAPTER 5

I NEVER IMAGINED that within weeks of my separation from Chai I would be offered a job entertaining high-class Japanese businessmen. It happened quite by accident.

The bar I was working in on Surawong Road was close to the red-light district called Soi Thaniya. This area caters to the *nihonjin*—the Japanese. These *nihonjin* pay a fortune for Thai hostesses to chat, drink, and sing karaoke with them. Sophisticated-looking women in evening gowns, short dresses, and kimonos call out '*Irashaimase*' (meaning 'Welcome') to any passer-by who looks Japanese. This place is otherwise known as Japantown and is considered a utopia by its many male customers. The bars were all on good terms with the police, so it was a safe area.

The bar I worked in was often visited by groups of *nihonjin* in search of fun. I never took any notice of them because I couldn't speak their language; I found it too complex and altogether unfathomable. Personally, I prefer to mix with *farang*s, as I find them more fun and less formal.

When my boss called me aside one day to tell me that a Japanese businessman had expressed an interest in me, I was flabbergasted. I knew the man he was referring to because he had visited the bar several times that week. I had smiled at him and occasionally allowed him to chat to me; I understood very little of what he said, but I would nod my head in agreement at what I thought to be the appropriate junctures in conversation, or smile agreeably from time to time.

The bar was owned by Ichiro, another Japanese expatriate, who nursed a stereotypical love of beer, karaoke, and sushi.

'Be smart, Bua,' he advised me. 'You will sit with Hiroshi and keep him entertained whenever he visits.'

In return, he promised to pay me commission on every drink Hiroshi ordered. In simpler terms, I was getting paid to smile sweetly and nod my head.

Hiroshi was at least 30 years my senior. I didn't find him physically attractive; on the contrary, he reminded me of Saddam Hussein because he looked more middle-eastern than *nihonjin*. This was probably because of the tan he'd achieved from golfing under the Thai sun.

On the first night I was to entertain him, he appeared at the bar and summoned me to his side to have a drink with him. I did as Ichiro had instructed me and greeted him like a long-lost friend.

'*Sabai dee mai*, Hiroshi*san*.'

He responded in Thai, but his pronunciation was unintelligible. Of course, I smiled and pretended to understand him. The waiter came over to our table with a tray containing a flask of sake and a square, wooden cup. I poured the sake into the cup, filling it to the brim to signify prosperity. He stared at me as he sipped the drink. I was wary that another girl might try to catch his attention so I tried to maintain eye contact with him. He had a hungry look in his eyes as they lowered to take in the rest of my body. His gaze lingered over my legs and breasts until he had satisfied his hunger.

What followed was a drunken flirtation that lasted several hours. He complimented me on my beauty several times and patted my thigh suggestively. He was boisterous and loud and did most of the talking, leaving me to just smile agreeably.

Moments before the bar closed for the night, he asked me if I was a virgin. Although he was drunk, he was still lucid enough to understand the implications of asking such a question. I knew it was common for Japanese men to take mistresses, or what they called *aijin*. I lied and told him that my virtue was still intact. My answer had been an instinctive thing, but it both surprised and alarmed me. It was a small and simple lie, yet one that carried a lot of weight; it suggested a willingness to go down a path I had previously never dreamed I would step foot on.

Hiroshi smiled at my reply. He didn't ask me to sleep with him that night. He stood up, waved goodbye to Ichiro, and wished me goodnight. He returned the following night and beckoned me to his side. This time, he didn't waste any time with pleasantries. He addressed me in Thai to ensure that I understood what he meant.

'*Pai yoo kub pom mai?*'

I was speechless. Hiroshi wanted me to move into an apartment he owned. I felt shyness envelop me, but his warm smile helped to put me at ease.

'Hiroshi, you shouldn't tease me with such offers.'

But he assured me he was not joking.

'You can play the innocent girl with me if you wish, but I understand girls like you.'

With that he called to the waiter for more sake, and then changed the topic of conversation. I knew that this was his way of giving me some time to consider the proposal.

I couldn't help but recall Chai and all the pain I had suffered during our brief marriage. I was wary of getting into another relationship so soon after him. Hiroshi was wealthy beyond belief, but I was new to this world and, in my naivety, I didn't realise the significance of this. It was only after I had politely declined his offer that I realised how envious the other girls were of me. It was their ultimate goal to meet a rich man who could take care of them. If there was even a hint of wealth about a customer, all of the girls in the bar would flock around him, fiercely competing with one another to catch his eye. I would soon learn the tricks of the trade and become much more astute, but for now I was still innocent.

Hiroshi interpreted my rejection as a sign that I was different to the other girls. We developed an unlikely friendship. He would come to the bar every night, sing karaoke, and drink sake until he was so drunk he could no longer stand. I think that he also fooled himself into believing that I was just playing hard to get, and he seemed more than prepared to do plenty of chasing. He visited me every night, after he had finished work for the day, and he was usually laden down with gifts.

Although I had nothing but platonic feelings for Hiroshi, I did flirt with him; I saw it as a small trade-off for maintaining the money his patronage provided. Hiroshi, in turn, saw his gifts as money well-spent as they helped him assert a false sense of ownership. Knowing he had good connections in Japantown, I decided to ask Hiroshi to find me a better job. I had no idea what he had in mind for me.

His friend owned a bar called Jasmine's on Soi Thaniya, and I agreed to work there on the assumption that I would be behind the bar. I had no idea that I was soon to become a commodity, a product to be picked out and paid for. When I presented myself to the manageress, or what we called the *mamasan*, she immediately requested that I change out of the outfit I arrived in and into a silk dress with a blue tag with '34' written on it.

I looked confusedly at Hiroshi, who was standing nearby, but he waved his hand as if to dismiss my concerns.

'Pay no attention to her, *mamasan*,' he said. 'I know this girl and she is grateful for the opportunity you are giving her.'

'Hiroshi…' I started to say but he interrupted me by gently nudging me into the dressing room.

'You are here to entertain me and nothing else. Don't be foolish Bua. Do you think I would deceive you?'

In the dressing room the other girls assured me that Hiroshi had arranged for me to work there in order to prevent other men from meeting me. He would be able to control who I spent my time with, and who I was allowed to speak to. I trusted that he cared about me, so this seemed like a plausible suggestion, although I was vaguely uncomfortable with being brought into a world where women were lined up like pieces of jewellery that men could select as they wished—even if we were just providing company to them.

BEFORE I TURNED 19, I had accidentally become a hostess and would spend the following seven years working at Jasmine's. Every night, I lined up with the other girls, smiling graciously at the patrons who selected, with *mamasan*'s help and recommendation, which one of us he wanted to be his hostess for the night. My situation in Jasmine's was unusual compared to other hostesses because *mamasan* was told to keep me available for Hiroshi alone. She always informed me of Hiroshi's arrival, and I would join him at his table immediately, regardless of who I was entertaining at the time.

Hiroshi proved to be the caring man I had first believed him to be. He did everything in his power to make my life as enjoyable as possible. He showered me with money and attention during his pursuit of my affections. I saw him as my guardian; someone who gently guided me in life, but who also allowed me considerable freedom. He paid handsomely for my company, but he generally permitted me to talk to other clients if he was not present, allowing me to earn commission on the drinks they ordered. I earned 80 baht in commission for every drink they bought. Besides the drinks commission, I earned a fixed wage of 8,000 baht a month and Hiroshi never failed to tip me 500 baht each night that I accompanied him.

In fact, the Japanese were easy to work with because I didn't have to ask if they would like to order a drink. Once I sat with a client, a waiter instantly came with a tray of drinks and put a glass of cola in front of me, which would also earn me commission. Japanese men knew what was expected of them and were very generous with money. I rarely had to ask them to buy me a drink.

Still, I dared not think what would happen to me if Hiroshi's opinion of me ever changed or if he discovered that I was not a virgin, but the mother of a young child.

Months passed by while Hiroshi and I followed this same routine of late-night drinking, flirting, and cavorting. Then one night he arrived at the bar with a Japanese woman.

'Bua, this is my wife,' he said by way of introduction.

My breath caught and I couldn't bring myself to say anything.

'*Mai pen rai*, Bua. It's all right, she knows all about you.'

My first thought was that this woman was jealous and had come to the bar to confront me. But her expression was blank. She was polite to me and remained impassive, even when Hiroshi introduced me as his *aijin*. I was a little embarrassed by his crudeness, but she nodded in approval and bowed to me politely. I returned the gesture.

'*Kombanwa watashi wa* Bua *desu*,' I said, formally introducing myself in Japanese.

She smiled, which unnerved me slightly, all the time maintaining a courteous expression.

I accompanied Hiroshi and his wife to a table where I waited on them for the evening. If she despised me, she did an excellent job of concealing it, and she maintained her composure for the duration of the night.

When they finally decided to leave, she approached me and bowed once again. I returned the courtesy. It was then that I realised she did not feel threatened by me. She had probably known of my existence for some time, although I must confess that I hadn't known of hers—I had deliberately not asked Hiroshi about that aspect of his life.

Hiroshi returned to Jasmine's alone the following night. He sat in his usual seat and ordered a drink. I sat down beside him and he could tell straight away that I was angry.

'Sit with me, girl. There are some things that you do not understand,' he said.

'I am Japanese. My wife knows that I have a Thai girlfriend. I am a man. My wife and I lead separate lives.'

He went on to explain that his wife lived in Japan with the children, while he lived in Thailand. He hadn't been back to Japan in a long time, and she only rarely came to Thailand. I had witnessed first-hand his wife's strange acceptance of the situation the previous night, so I knew that he was not lying.

'That is the end of the matter. We will speak no more of my wife,' he said, as he stroked my thigh.

THOUGH I ENJOYED Hiroshi's attention, as time passed, it became a little too routine. He would visit me at the bar every night, arriving between 7pm and 8pm, and leaving at 1am. I occasionally met other men, but Hiroshi ensured that developing a relationship with any of them was out of the question. His patronage secured me a luxurious lifestyle; I regularly dined at five-star restaurants and spent his money on extravagant shopping sprees. The other girls at Jasmine's found his behaviour almost incomprehensible. He was spending all this money on me, and yet I still refused to become his mistress.

I, however, knew what attracted him. The truth was that he was not really in love with me, but simply saw my coy 'innocence' as a challenge. Though I never responded to his advances, he did everything in his power to make me feel special and loved. He declared his undying love for me on a daily basis, and begged me to put him out of his misery and become his mistress. He asked me when I would give in to his demands, but I refused to answer.

His influence on my life extended beyond the bar where I worked. In time, I introduced Hiroshi to *mae*, to whom he began sending money every month. He even sent her souvenirs from countries that he visited on his business trips. Though he was older than *mae* and she must have been suspicious of our relationship, she never asked any questions.

All of my friends in the bar envied my arrangement with Hiroshi. They regarded his patronage as essentially money for nothing.

I wasn't Hiroshi's first Thai girlfriend. He had supported several girls and their families before me, though all of these relationships had ended when he discovered they had been unfaithful. I came to conclude that his interest in me was fuelled by his obsession with my virginity; he was still blissfully unaware of the fact that I had lost it long ago.

Sometimes, when I was feeling daring, I would ask Hiroshi why he continued to pursue me.

'Why do you come here everyday? I want to talk to other clients, too, you know.'

He would smile at me dismissively, as if dealing with a spoilt child. He wasn't accustomed to hearing a girl talk to him in such a disrespectful way.

He showered me with gifts of Japanese jewellery. In the beginning, I assumed that these were precious gifts he wished to bestow on his precious girlfriend. But in time I discovered that he was hesitant to give me Thai jewellery in case

I sold it—foreign gold commanded a poor price in Bangkok.

Like all Japanese men, Hiroshi was careful to adopt a long-term strategy for success. This is perhaps why he waited three years before asking me to accompany him on a holiday to Chiang Mai, in northern Thailand, for three days and two nights. I suspected that he wanted to consummate our relationship and, even though I had no desire to be physically intimate with him, I agreed to go. Besides, I had come to the gradual conclusion that Hiroshi enjoyed the chase more than anything else.

We had to take a flight to Chiang Mai, a city surrounded by tall mountains. Once there, Hiroshi was keen to visit as many mountain temples as possible, whilst I, on the other hand, was content to visit just the one—a temple called Wat Prathat Doi Suthep, which overlooks the city of Chiang Mai. It is situated on the top of a mountain and accessed by endless steps. Two magnificent, seven-headed *naga* (serpents) slide down the sides of the steps, serving as banisters.

At the summit, there was a *chedi*, which contained the relics of Buddha, but no woman, regardless of her status, was permitted to enter its inner sanctum. This was because the relics rested below the baseline of the *chedi*, and the monks feared menstruating women would taint its holiness.

Despite this, the visit proved a very special and memorable one. Had it not been for his age, I might even have fallen in love with Hiroshi.

When darkness fell, a chauffeur collected us and drove us to the hotel.

I pretended to be unaware of his intentions on the first night, so when Hiroshi took me to a club and spent the evening buying cocktails and champagne, I made sure to pace my drinks, so I was still quite sober when we returned to the hotel.

I accompanied Hiroshi to his room. He closed the door behind me with a satisfied grin. This was the moment he'd been waiting for. He moved to touch me, but I slithered free from his grip with the agility of a snake.

'No, leave me alone,' I said to him.

'Don't be so ungrateful Bua.'

His face fell as I resolutely grabbed a blanket and lay down on the floor.

'What are you doing? Don't worry, I've got condoms. I'm prepared.'

'I'm not,' I replied. 'I'm drunk and tired. Do not disrespect me again! Goodnight.'

And with that I went to sleep.

I awoke the following morning to face a disgruntled Hiroshi. His hopes of taking my virginity had been dashed. I didn't expect him to take rejection well, but he surprised me by quickly returning to his normal good-humoured self.

That evening, after visits to more temples, he took me to another club where I made a point of befriending a girl whom I urged Hiroshi to entertain. I was hoping that she would serve as a distraction and I wouldn't have to fight Hiroshi off if we spent the night drinking with her.

In my reckless insolence, I invited her back to the hotel with us. At first, Hiroshi didn't object and the girl accompanied us back to the room. But as Hiroshi began to sober up he realised that I had been leading him on all these years, with no intention of ever sleeping with him. He was furious. He raised his voice to me for the first time and accused me of embarrassing him and making him feel smaller than anyone else had managed to do in his entire life.

He bid our guest goodnight and went to his bed without saying another word to me. He didn't try to seduce me again that night or any other night.

He had visited the club every evening for three years, but that holiday was to mark the end of our friendship.

It was only when I received my salary that I noticed his patronage had ceased.

In the years that followed, I often wondered why I hadn't ever relented to his incessant pleas that I become his mistress. But deep down I knew that the answer to this question was really quite simple; he knew nothing of my child or my marriage, and had I let myself become emotionally attached to Hiroshi, there would have been a greater risk of my secrets being exposed. Such an exposure would have doomed our relationship, and his patronage, to an even more hostile closure.

I saw Hiroshi once more after that holiday, and I took the opportunity to ask him why he had vanished.

'To be honest Bua, I've met another girl, a university student,' he told me.

'Is she a real student?' I asked.

'Yes. I'm paying for her courses and she shows me her report cards. I couldn't wait for you anymore. A man has his needs, you must know that.'

I have to admit that I felt a little jealous of his new relationship. My own insecurities, rather than any strong emotions for Hiroshi, gnawed away at me. I wondered if his feelings for this girl were more genuine than they had been for me, or if he thought her intellectually superior to me because she was a university student.

I never saw Hiroshi again, and it was only in later years that I realised the stupidity of my actions. He had supported me for over three years, and when our relationship ended I was told by *mamasan* that I might have to entertain other clients if it was asked of me. Apparently the bar was losing business to rival establishments whose hostesses offered their customers what *mamasan* politely called a 'more flexible service'.

Jasmine's was to offer a 'ten drinks' option, a code word for the bar fine patrons would have to pay to take a hostess away from the premises. The 700 baht fine went entirely to the bar. How much a hostess would earn for service outside the bar was decided by her, and belonged to her. It ranged from 3,000 baht for a 'short time' to 6,000 baht for an overnight stay. We hostesses were told that we would be given red number tags instead of blue ones, because red meant you were available for sale. However, *mamasan* assured us that none of us would be forced to do anything against our will. Her assistants would approach the clients and offer the new service by gesturing to a girl and asking them if they wanted to go to a hotel with her.

This new policy came as no surprise to me because I knew long before that some of my co-workers had secretly sold their bodies to the clients. It was only a matter of time before Jasmine's would have to embrace prostitution. This new status was mutually beneficial because the bar earned more money in bar fines, and the girls who already sold themselves didn't need to hide anymore.

I wasn't interested in prostitution because I was too shy and sexually inexperienced.

Surprisingly, *mamasan* seemed to accept my position and agreed that I would offer only the services of a drinking companion. Although I was not yet having to prostitute myself, I found myself sinking deeper and deeper into the murky world where women were no more than objects to be bought.

It was much easier to allow myself to sink further, than to fight my way out.

CHAPTER 6

I OFTEN ASK myself why I permitted Hiroshi to exit my life so abruptly. I had managed to convince myself that he was an unnecessary distraction, but it was only when he was gone that I realised how much I missed him. He had been a true friend and guardian to me for a long time. The change in my fortunes was noticeable at once, and I became just like any of the other girls. I had never known what it was like to have to desperately seek patronage from customers because Hiroshi had always been there for me in the past.

I knew that any chance of a comfortable life had vanished along with Hiroshi. I bitterly regretted the way I had treated him. I had strung him along for over three years, accepting his gifts even though I had known all along that he wouldn't be content with simply holding my hand forever.

The loss of his patronage meant that I was no longer able to afford my room and was forced to move into a small wooden house located in a hidden slum on Charoen Krung Road. The rent for this privilege was 2,000 baht a month, and the house was nothing more than an old shack.

I was now stuck with a job with no real sense of purpose and absolutely no prospects; hostessing usually just serves as a stepping stone into prostitution. I was perhaps the only hostess at Jasmine's who did not sleep with her customers.

Although I was not actively involved in the sex industry, it was like wallpaper in my day-to-day life, and I had effectively become desensitised to it.

I would occasionally invite friends, who worked as prostitutes, to my home. We would spend such nights drinking beer and talking about men, clients, and how much money they earned.

What little money I had, I squandered on alcohol in an effort to escape the harsh reality I had been plunged into. I drank both at home and in the bars and clubs of Ratchadapisek, a district in Bangkok that is renowned for its debauchery and decadence. There was no problem in life that couldn't be washed away with a couple of cheap beers. Rather than admit to myself that I had completely lost my way in life, I instead likened alcohol to pain medicine. If you had a headache, you took a painkiller. And if you had a problem, what was wrong with using alcohol to numb this type of pain?

It was at this time, when I was at my lowest, that I fell in love for the first time. His name was Yuth, and he was a motorcycle courier. I met him by chance in a bar while drinking with friends. He was a year or two older than I and was more attractive than Chai. To others, he had a tendency to act like a beer-swilling macho man, quick to verbally abuse anyone that glanced in his direction. But to me, he was sweet and affectionate. I refused to acknowledge any of his faults, happier to focus on his charming and exciting nature.

Yuth and I shared a mutual friend, Som, who invited us on a double date with her and her boyfriend Pira. I agreed without hesitation, eager for an opportunity to see Yuth. We decided to go to a movie. After ages of deliberating over what to wear, I finally settled on a silk dress that revealed only a modest amount of cleavage.

On the night of the date, we met in a bar close to the cinema. At first, the conversation between Yuth and me was slightly awkward.

But as we both began to relax, we became increasingly flirtatious.

We didn't hold hands in the cinema, but later, as we made our way to the restaurant, I felt him place his hand on the small of my back.

He sat beside me at the dinner table, and our two friends sat opposite us. Conversation revolved around our jobs, the people we knew, and Jasmine's.

My friend Som spoke openly in front of her boyfriend about working as an escort, and joked about how much she was able to earn.

I drank a lot that evening, emboldened by Yuth, who repeatedly topped up my glass, no doubt hoping it would lower my guard.

After dinner, Som and Pira left, leaving Yuth and me alone. Taking advantage of the privacy, Yuth immediately leaned forward and whispered, 'What would you like to do now?'

His question caught me by surprise; Thai men are usually not so forward.

He mentioned that he knew I worked in Jasmine's, implying that he believed I, like my friend Som, sold my body. I was about to set him straight, but as before, when Hiroshi had asked me if I was a virgin, instinct took over and I found myself silently agreeing.

Yuth assured me that he didn't have a problem with prostitution, before whispering in my ear, 'You must be a wonderful lover.'

These words struck me with the force of a bolt of lightening. I reached for his hand to steady myself as I stood up. We made our way outside, where he began to kiss me passionately to the astonishment of passers-by, who raised their hands to their mouths in an expression of disbelief. In Thailand, public displays of affection are considered *na mai ai*; they are shameful.

But Yuth didn't care, and sought only to shock them further by shouting, 'What are you looking at? Have you never seen lovers before?'

I giggled, thrilled by his nonchalance. I loved his tiger attitude to life, the taste of beer and cigarettes on his lips, and the way he held me close. No one had ever kissed me with such passion before.

It took us ten minutes to reach a cheap motel. He paid the fee for the room, before almost pushing me through the doorway in his excitement.

'Now you're mine,' he declared triumphantly, as I began to undress. He took off his shirt and pushed me onto the bed.

We both struggled to remove our clothes, our haste and excitement causing zippers to catch and shirts and dresses to become tangled.

When we were finally standing naked before one another, I leaned forward and whispered in Yuth's ear, 'I'm all yours.'

He lay me down on the bed and climbed on top of me, frothing at the mouth like a wild animal. Five minutes later I climaxed in his arms.

For the first time in my life, I'd had sex with someone I actually felt an attraction to.

A period of blissful courting and passion followed that first night. We became inseparable, like siamese twins. My feelings were reciprocated as Yuth told me that, for him, this was *ruk thae*, or true love.

Only a week into our courtship he introduced me to his mother, and a week later he moved into my shack. His mother and sister moved into a neighbouring shack shortly afterwards. We were moving at breakneck speed, but I figured love was supposed to be reckless, and so I had no desire to slow things down.

Our roller-coaster affair climbed to a dizzying height before dramatically derailing one evening several weeks after we first met.

My friends and I decided to go to Khorat to watch a solar eclipse after work one evening, but I neglected to tell Yuth of my plan. I returned to Bangkok a few days later and was working in Jasmine's when he came looking for me. He approached me from behind and laid his hand roughly on my shoulder as I stood in the bar. I jumped in fright because I knew a customer would never dare touch a girl in such a fashion. When I turned around, Yuth grabbed me by the shoulders and started to shake me as he screamed, 'We are leaving right now.'

His breath reeked of alcohol and his eyes were alight with a fire that was all too familiar from my time with Chai.

As soon as we had reached my shack and he had closed the door on the rest of the world, he beat me senseless.

'Where were you? Who were you with?' he demanded, viciously striking me between each question.

I told him the truth—that I had simply gone home to Khorat to watch the eclipse. My eyes began to well up with tears, but rather than feel pity for me, he took this as an admission of guilt.

'You lying whore!'

He began slapping me across the face with both hands. I was too shocked to defend myself. All I could do was repeat the words, 'This cannot be happening to me, this cannot be happening to me,' over and over in my head in a vain attempt to focus on anything other than his pummelling fists.

He continued to scream obscenities with every slap, punch, and kick he dealt me. The noise eventually brought worried neighbours to our door. One of these neighbours was Yuth's mother.

'Leave her alone for the sake of your mother,' she pleaded with him through the closed door. But her words couldn't penetrate Yuth's steely rage.

'This is none of your business! Stay out of it!' He screamed in unison with another swift blow to my stomach that caused me to fall to my knees, gasping for breath.

'Don't fuck with me bitch,' he screamed as he began to circle me. He kicked me one last time, then turned and walked out of the house, his head held defiantly high as he marched past his mother and the rest of the neighbours that had assembled.

His mother helped me to my feet.

'I'm sorry. I prayed that you would never have to deal with his temper. He just can't seem to help himself when he starts drinking. His father was the same.'

I started sobbing in her arms, and she stroked my hair like I was a small child. I had done nothing to provoke him—I was completely innocent. But I had played this game with Chai so many times before that I should have known that there were no rules and that justice certainly wasn't a contender.

Yuth's mother took me back to her shack where she helped me get cleaned up. An hour later I ventured back to my house. Yuth was no longer conscious. He was snoring peacefully on the couch. I tiptoed by him and went straight to bed.

When he awoke from his drunken slumber the next morning, he was still angry.

'If you ever do that again, I will beat the living daylights out of you, bitch,' he snarled.

When I left Chai, I vowed never to let another man strike me. Yet here I was again: walking on eggshells, terrified that one would crack and alert Yuth to my presence. I thought that if I could just make myself invisible then I would be safe. But sometimes the loudest sound in the world is someone trying their very hardest to be silent.

During the following weeks, I began to realise that I had not known Yuth at all. I only discovered that he had a criminal record for theft and assault when I happened to open the door to his parole officer one afternoon. When pressed, his mother confessed that he had served five years in Klong Pai Prison in Nakhon Ratchasima. Our whirlwind courtship had left me so dizzy that I was unable to focus on anything other than how amazing he made me feel, and so the plain, cold facts that had been staring me in the face had gotten lost in all the commotion.

But the honeymoon period had come to an abrupt end. Yuth had taken off his mask and revealed himself to be just another Chai—an angry and jealous man.

I knew that, like Chai, he would never change, but his mother begged and pleaded with me not to leave him. She even told me that I could earn merit from Buddha if I tried to help Yuth. Rather than interpret this as a form of spiritual blackmail, I simply saw her as a mother desperate to save her son from himself.

Unfortunately I could no more control Yuth's behaviour than he seemed able to. His mood swings and jealousy were independent of alcohol, making him all the more unpredictable. He was also a master of deceit. After he beat me for the first time, he confessed that he had lost his job some weeks ago. At first I didn't believe him, as he had been leaving for work every afternoon since we had moved in together. He laughed at my confusion and seemed to consider this deceit a personal triumph against me.

'I spent each day drinking in bars with my friends, while you thought I was at work,' he boasted, as I stared on in disbelief at the stranger standing before me.

There were times when I thought of leaving Yuth, but I stayed because I was still in love with the man I had met on our first date. I convinced myself that even if this man never resurfaced, he was still in there somewhere, and just the memory of him alone made the beatings more tolerable. It became my mission to retain the love Yuth had once professed for me. I was willing to forsake a comfortable home and put up with the physical abuse once I had someone who loved me as much as I loved him; the fact that I was in love with a ghost was irrelevant. This, of course, made sense to no one else but me.

Throughout my life, I had always believed that unforeseen powers shaped my fate and that I must have committed some terrible deed in a previous life, for which I was now paying the price. This belief was compounded three months later when I fell pregnant with Yuth's child. I had been on the pill, so the news came as a complete surprise.

My first thought was that I had to have an abortion. I already had one child in this world that I was unable to take care of, and I couldn't bear the idea of having a second baby in identical circumstances to the first.

I approached Yuth's mother in the strictest of confidence and asked for her help. I knew that it would be a difficult situation for her because she secretly longed for a grandchild.

At first, she pleaded with me to reconsider the termination. But when she realised I wasn't going to change my mind, she reluctantly offered the name of a Chinese pharmacist who might be able to help me.

Although abortion is illegal in Thailand, backstreet services are available to women who find themselves in my situation.

I presented myself at the pharmacist's shop the following morning. There were no customers there at the time, and that instantly relaxed me. An old Chinese man stood behind the counter waiting to serve me.

'I want *yaa kub leaud*.'

'You want something to take your baby out?' he asked.

I nodded, unsettled by his bluntness. He casually removed his spectacles and cleaned the lenses with a handkerchief before asking, 'How far along are you?'

I told him I was in my second month. He turned his back to me and began rummaging through dozens of small drawers containing all sorts of mysterious-looking ingredients.

Moments later, he handed me what looked like powder wrapped in paper.

'Take this with a glass of water and drink it in one gulp.'

When I reached my trembling hand forward to take the package from him, he lent over the counter and whispered, 'No refund. If it doesn't work, don't bother coming here again.'

I nodded and paid him the 2,000 baht fee.

I had not told Yuth my news for obvious reasons, so when I returned home to find him busy mending a broken door, I hurried past on the pretence that I needed to use the toilet.

Once inside the bathroom, I sat on the floor and laid the abortion medicine on the ground in front of me, and began to do battle with my conscience.

I spoke to my unborn baby.

I'm sorry. I'm not ready to have you. I hope that you can forgive me.

I rubbed my belly and asked Buddha to forgive me for the life that I was about to take, and with that I swallowed the potion.

If there really is a next life, I hope you will be reborn as my child.

The potion had a bitter taste and left my throat feeling ticklish for hours afterwards. I went and lay down on my bed, unsure of what to expect. The Chinese man had told me that if I saw blood soon after drinking the potion, I would know it had worked. I waited and waited, but nothing happened.

Later that afternoon, I made dinner and cleaned the house, all the while feeling perfectly fine, physically if not emotionally.

I went to bed that night knowing that the potion had not worked and that I would soon become a mother again. I felt ashamed and wondered if I had harmed my child. I prayed to the baby to forgive me and vowed never to let the word 'abortion' escape from my lips again.

When I finally mustered up the courage to tell Yuth, he was initially pleased by the news. But this soon changed when he realised that, as was customary in such circumstances, I would have to give up work. He had grown accustomed to drinking all day with his friends while I kept the roof over our heads. The impending arrival of a baby is supposed to bring joy into a home, but in our case it turned the rift that had arisen between Yuth and me into a chasm.

Though it had been seven years since I had first started working at Jasmine's, I had saved only a mere 20,000 baht.

Yuth refused to look for work, and so we were forced to rely on his mother to feed and support us, even though she was poor and already struggling just to support herself. She somehow managed to put aside 100 baht a day for me to use for food. She also brought me leftovers from food offerings she had scavenged at the local temple where she worked as a funeral florist. My sister also gave me what little money she could afford. Yuth contributed nothing.

My second child was a boy and I called him Atid. To my relief, he was born healthy despite the potion that I had consumed. I figured this meant that he must have committed a lot of good deeds in his past lives.

Yuth had become temporarily less violent during my pregnancy; however, he reverted to his old ways after the birth. If the baby cried at night, he would blame me and subject me to a beating as my punishment.

He treated my body like an inanimate piece of flesh, rolling on top of me whenever he felt like having sex, and beating me into submission if I dared move a muscle in protest.

It was during one such incident that he got me pregnant again. This time, the thought of an abortion didn't even cross my mind. The baby was a girl, whom I called Peung.

I became convinced that she possessed magical powers because Yuth was transfixed by her from the moment she was born. His old tenderness resurfaced in the way he dedicated himself to Peung's care. He treated her as though she were the most precious gem in the world.

Part of this tenderness spread to me, as he also stopped beating me for a while. His transformation, although temporary, was one from a tiger into a mouse. And although our relationship improved as a result, our financial situation did not.

While Yuth seemed indifferent to our poverty, I desperately wanted more, if not for myself and Yuth, then at least for our children. I didn't want their childhoods to be fenced in and restricted by the poverty that had plagued my own youth. It was a disease that I had struggled with into adulthood, and I feared that history was about to repeat itself.

I had planned to return to work at Jasmine's after Peung was born, but I was worried it would upset Yuth. When our situation began to reach crisis proportions, I was left with no other option.

I had not visited the bar since giving birth to my last two children. I had also lost touch with the girls I used to work with. I discussed the idea with Yuth, who had yet to find any regular employment. Although he was initially against it, he was unable to offer an alternative solution.

When I returned to Japantown, Jasmine's was gone and another bar stood on its premises.

Thaniya Street had changed very little. It was a little cleaner now and better organised.

I walked the street, peering through the windows of the different bars. Every one of them was advertising for hostesses.

Female candidates wanted, between 18-25. No experience needed.

Though I knew these advertisements were in fact invitations to work as prostitutes, I was so desperate for money that I considered applying. I could no longer afford to buy clothes for my children, and I lay awake at night worrying about how I would feed them in the morning. I also had a lazy, unemployed partner to feed. Selling my body seemed to be the only option that would bring in enough money to solve my problems.

In that moment, with all these worries rushing through my head, I impulsively walked into the nearest bar. A woman I guessed to be the *mamasan* came over to greet me.

I asked if there were any vacancies and explained that I had worked in Jasmine's.

The *mamasan* was younger than others I had met in the past. I could instantly tell from her demeanour that she was not interested in me.

'Unfortunately,' she said, 'the only position going is for that of a hostess. What age are you?'

'I am 29.'

'That's a pity. You are probably too old.'

I knew it wasn't personal. Thaniya *mamasan*s are known for their courteous manner, and she explained as kindly as she could that she permitted only girls aged between 18 and 25 to work as consorts.

'Our Japanese customers prefer girls of this age.'

I thanked her for her kindness. I waited until I was outside of the bar before breaking down and weeping uncontrollably.

Every time I closed my eyes all I could see was my small, defenceless little Peung. At the time, she was just nine months old. Her brother Atid was only a year older.

A man stopped me on the street to ask if I needed help, but I ignored him and walked away. What could I say? I was too old to work as a hostess. My future looked bleak.

CHAPTER 7

I BELIEVE IN karma, and it is this belief that has helped me to come to terms with the brutality and poverty that has been so prominent in my life. The basic concept of karma revolves around the law of cause and effect—for every action there is a reaction. We are the sum total of our actions, past and present, and it is the nature of these actions that determines the pain or joy we experience in each life. I had come to the conclusion that I must have done some terrible deeds in a past life to warrant such a turbulent present.

It is difficult for anyone who has not experienced true poverty to empathise with the full horror of such a life. It's like being a mere shadow of a human being; the outline has been drawn but you're still waiting to be coloured in. The only thing that reassures you that you are in fact alive is the gnawing hunger in your belly and the constant worries about food, clothes, and bills that consume your waking hours.

My children went to bed hungry every night and cried themselves to sleep. I sacrificed as much of my own food portions as I could to try to fill their shrinking stomachs. But there was never enough. Yuth would sit alongside us at the dinner table with downturned eyes; I couldn't remember the last time he had helped pay for even the most basic of necessities.

We relied heavily on his mother, who would willingly sacrifice her own meals just to feed her beloved grandchildren.

My days were spent searching for ways to earn some money. I had lost the luxury of being picky and was willing to take up any employment that would bring an end to the present misery. It was around this time, when my guard was down and I was truly desperate, that the opportunity to engage in prostitution presented itself.

Contrary to what most people believe, it is usually women who recruit other women into vice. Gaining face plays an important role in the recruitment strategy. Parents boast about how they have bought a new house on money their daughters have sent them every month, although they fail to mention how it is earned. Neighbours who want to keep up then encourage their daughters to work in prostitution to make equal amounts of money. In Thailand, children are expected to be grateful to their parents. Men can earn merit on behalf of their parents by becoming monks, while women sell their bodies to feed their parents' materialistic craze. Bar girls often make trips home, not only to pay respect to their parents, but also to persuade other women to join in the business, thereby earning commission.

In my case, I was not fooled into selling my body by a pimp; the offer came from a woman I met in the local vegetable market.

Her name was Nok, and she worked as a go-go dancer in Patpong, the most infamous red-light district in Bangkok. I had known her for years, and although everyone in the slum knew what she did for a living, it was not openly discussed.

We met by chance in the market one Saturday afternoon. Spotting Peung and me poring over the various vegetables, she came over to say hello. Peung was just beginning to learn how to arrange words from her limited vocabulary into a relatively intelligible sentence, and she provided Nok and me with ample entertainment. Nok enquired after Yuth, and we made small talk about the various mutual acquaintances we had. A more serious undercurrent soon developed as conversation turned to Jasmine's and my current predicament. I asked Nok where she was working, careful to keep my tone casual.

'I am leaving my job,' she told me, 'I am moving home to work on my parents' farm. It will be a new life.'

Nok was an Isan native from the Nakhon Phanom province. She and her husband were childless, but they hoped to start a family when they returned to the northeast.

'Maybe,' I ventured, 'you could call me if the club requires new staff.'

A look of surprise flitted across her face. She had known me a long time and I had never before expressed any interest in getting involved in prostitution. She realised that I hadn't been exaggerating how bad my situation was.

'I could get you a job. Come with me tonight if you want me to introduce you to the *mamasan*. Can you meet me this evening?' she asked me.

We both understood what the job would involve, but my main concern was exactly how much I could earn.

'The money is good if you work hard and earn commission from drinks,' she said, avoiding a direct answer.

I asked her exactly what would be expected of me, and once again she avoided alluding to the one aspect of the job we both knew I was referring to.

'The girls arrive for work an hour early to get their make-up done. We wear bikinis and boots, sometimes heels, and dance on the stage. It's not really like Jasmine's because most of the customers are *farang*s.'

I interrupted and asked her directly, 'Does the *mamasan* make you sleep with the customers?'

'No, it's up to you if you want to or not. I make 2,000 baht for a quickie…'

She suddenly paused, seeming disarmed by her own bluntness. She continued, 'My husband knows what I do, and he doesn't object so long as I never stay overnight with a client—not that I'd ever want to.'

She suggested that I accompany her to the bar and make up my own mind about the work.

I spent the walk home mulling things over, and by the end of the journey I had made up my mind. When I visited the bar with Nok that evening, it would be to secure employment. I couldn't afford the luxury of sitting around debating the merits of the job because essentially there was only one to consider—and that was the pay-packet.

I informed Yuth of my decision.

'Nok told me that her husband doesn't mind her servicing the customers as long as she doesn't stay overnight with them. She said that most of them ask for hand jobs only.'

His reply surprised me.

'Well, I suppose I don't mind either, so long as you don't go off with a Thai guy. Only *farang*s.'

I think I was secretly hoping that the thought of me being intimate with another man would incite a mixture of jealousy and chivalry in Yuth and he would rush to protect my virtue. In my imagined version of events, he would go to extremes to keep me from selling my body—an extreme in Yuth's case being that he would look for a job.

When the time came for me meet Nok, I said goodbye to Peung and Atid. They wrapped their little arms around me and buried their heads in the folds of my dress. Yuth managed to pry them away and gathered them up in his arms. I think children often have a sixth sense and know when something is wrong. Peung and Atid tried to squirm free of Yuth, stretching their arms out towards me in a plea to be brought along. Yuth seemed almost relieved by the distraction they afforded him and he busied himself with quietening them rather than having to look me in the eye.

'I'll be home in a few hours,' I promised them.

'I'll wait up,' I heard Yuth half-whisper as I closed the door behind me.

THE JOURNEY TO Soi Patpong took less than an hour. I met Nok at the bus stop, and we walked towards the red-light district. This area was a labyrinth of stalls, discos, restaurants, and brothels. The combination of decadence and debauchery was astonishing. Bar girls, prostitutes, and ladyboys decorated every street corner. They assumed their most seductive poses, arched their eyebrows, and pouted their lips the second a *farang* came within sight.

The ladyboys dressed far more provocatively than those I had occasionally seen in Japantown, and their figures and femininity were as pronounced as some of the prettiest girls I knew.

Hustlers and *mamasan*s loitered on the streets waving price lists and inviting tourists to see lewd ping-pong shows and live-sex acts.

'No cover charge, sir,' they would say in English, attempting to lure them in for a 'free' viewing. 'Take a look, sir. Welcome please.'

The place was teeming with *farang*s. I had never seen so many in the one place at the one time. Spirits were high, whether it was from alcohol or the sheer electricity of the atmosphere.

The *farang*s descended on the area to watch the lewd shows, drink beer and, above all else, have sex with Thai women.

Every colour of the rainbow shone down on the streets from the neon signs and the strobe lights of clubs. Giant screens advertised every commodity imaginable.

Whatever you were looking for, be it straight sex, ladyboys, swinging or S&M, you had come to the right place. No fetish was neglected and no fantasy left unfulfilled.

'Welcome to Patpong,' Nok said, smiling at my widened eyes. 'You'll get used to it,' she assured me.

We passed a boy riding a baby elephant that stood about five feet high. The *chang* reached out to me with its trunk and began rummaging through my pockets. Nok handed its owner 50 baht and she was given a small bag of popcorn in return. The elephant's trunk immediately made a grab for the treat, and it vanished into the cavern of his mouth. It then raised one leg, bowed its head and followed its owner up the street where they proceeded to repeat the trick.

The go-go bar where Nok danced was situated on the main *soi,* next to the lines of stalls that sold knick knacks and Thai souvenirs to tourists.

It was like nothing I had ever seen before. There were about 15 girls on a raised platform, holding onto poles and wearing identical uniforms that left nothing to the imagination: knee-high boots, thongs, and bikini tops. The bar ran along the outside of the stage, and the customers sat on stools around it, or watched the performances from small tables clustered nearby.

Each dancer was assigned a numbered badge which helped to identify her should a *farang* wish to single her out and request her company.

It was not the most glamorous club that I had ever visited; it was basically a brothel in disguise. I had anticipated the provocative dancing but not the level of nudity involved. The prospect of wearing such a revealing outfit made me feel instantly self-conscious. The dancers were all slimmer than me, with perkier bottoms and breasts. They were also all noticeably younger than me.

'This way Bua,' Nok said, guiding me into a room at the back of the club where I was introduced to the *mamasan*. Her name was Nhim and she used to be a bar girl. Rather than enquire about the pay or the working conditions, the first question that entered my head was what she thought of my bottom.

'Turn around girl,' she said. After an exaggerated sharp intake of breath, she exclaimed, 'You have a lovely tush, so learn how to shake it, as you've got competition for the customers. Show them you're as good as anyone else.'

I smiled not because I thought she was funny but because I was relieved.

'Now go get changed immediately. We're very busy.'

Nok then produced a thong and bikini top from her bag.

'These should fit you.'

I was about to ask Nok for directions to the changing room when I saw that she was already half undressed. This must be it I realised. I removed my clothes as the bar staff passed in and out of the room, but no one batted an eyelid.

'This is for you,' Nok said, handing me 2,000 baht. I realised that she had probably earned commission for recruiting me.

'It's your money. Use it for the children.'

I threw my arms around her and hugged her tightly.

'*Mai pen rai,*' she said in a croak-like voice that made me realise I was hugging her too tightly. 'You need it.'

FROM THE MOMENT I'd first arrived in the club, I was so overcome by the thought of having to dance on the stage that I hadn't had time to consider the even more terrifying prospect of being sold to a *farang*.

When I stepped out into the club in my thong and bikini top there were several girls dancing on the stage. I was about to climb onto the podium when Nok stopped me.

'The tall girls dance together and the short girls, like you and me, dance together. We usually swap over, from the back of the stage to the front, after every round of five songs. We'll work the clients until the changeover.'

Nok took me by the hand and guided me to a table beside the door where she explained to me that Nhim permitted only the most beautiful girls to dance at the front of the podium.

'She wants them on view so they will be immediately visible when a tourist looks through the door.'

I could feel the *mamasan's* eyes on me, so I gave Nok what I hoped was a confident smile. I was introduced to some of the girls who were flirting with customers at the bar, and when my name was called to the stage they pushed me forward to the front of the podium. I could see Nhim watching from the shadows. The butterflies in my stomach were doing aerial somersaults.

I had to share the stage with at least 15 other girls, so I found it hard to even move, let alone dance provocatively. But the *mamasan* was still watching me closely, so I tried to move as best I could to the rhythm of the awful dance music that filled the bar.

The club was soon crawling with *farang*s. They mingled with the girls and drank lots of beer. They cavorted with two or three girls at a time, yet still managed to keep an ever-watchful eye turned towards the stage. The atmosphere was hot and oppressive.

From the vantage point of the stage I noticed one *farang* in particular staring at me. Tall and bald, the white man sported sprawling tattoos, decorating the length and breadth of his arms. He was well-built and looked to be in his mid-thirties.

I saw him gesture to the *mamasan* and then whisper in her ear, all the while maintaining eye contact with me.

Nhim beckoned me over, and I gingerly stepped down from the podium and made my way over to her. The simple process of walking, placing one foot in front of the other, suddenly became extraordinarily difficult. My feet faltered with every step, and I teetered from side to side like a wounded dog. I affixed my broadest smile and tried to maintain eye contact with the westerner in the hope of distracting him from my trembling body. I wasn't sure how I was going to converse with him when I knew only a few words of English. I focused on such immediate obstacles because I wasn't ready just yet to contemplate the prospect of having sex with this stranger.

My efforts to disguise my nervousness had been in vain because when I reached his table, he smiled sympathetically at me and asked if I was alright. He guessed this was my first night. My paper-thin mask fell away instantly, and my terror was written all over my face. It was all I could do to remain standing. He informed Nhim that he would like to buy me. She could see how terrified I was so she leaned over and whispered in my ear.

'What's wrong dear? You're trembling like a newborn bird. Pull yourself together and go give him his money's worth.'

The westerner handed the *mamasan* 500 baht, which was the bar's fine to release me from work. Prostitution is illegal in Thailand, and so the bars can't actually charge customers to buy a girl out. They can only fine the customer for removing the girl from her work duties, which are simply to entertain the customers by dancing and to encourage them to buy drinks. It is then up to each girl to negotiate a fee directly with her client, which removes the bar from the picture completely.

He took me by the hand. I waved to Nok as we swept by her, but she had her hands full entertaining two *farang*s and didn't see me.

The *farang* never told me his name or asked for mine. When we left the red-light district he flagged a taxi and asked the driver to take us to a hotel in Din Daeng.

The hotel was beautiful—I had never seen such opulence before in my life. The *farang* took me straight to the bedroom, which was the size of my entire shack; in fact even the bed itself would have given my shack a run for its money. Thai furnishings and artefacts decorated the walls, and the carpet was so plush it wrapped around my feet like velvety quicksand.

He poured me a drink from the mini-bar. He sat back on the bed and smiled encouragingly at me.

'How old are you?' he asked.

I understood what he had said but in my nervousness the few English words that I had became scrambled.

When he realised that I couldn't communicate, he decided to switch to gestures and signs instead. He beckoned for me to follow him into the bathroom, where he proceeded to turn on the shower. I interpreted this as an instruction for me to wash. He sat watching as I undressed, but left the room when I stepped under the water. On my return the *farang* excused himself and took his turn in the bathroom.

I stood in the middle of the bedroom with a small bathrobe wrapped around me. I wasn't sure what to do next—should I wait here in my robe, or should I take it off and climb into bed? Did this man prefer to be in control or would he like me to take the initiative? My mind was swarming with questions as I had absolutely no idea what to expect—in fact Nok had warned me earlier that night to expect the unexpected.

In the end, I tentatively climbed under the bed covers. My heart was beating so loudly that I was convinced the *farang* could hear it through the closed door of the bathroom.

I wished that I could reach out and hit the pause button on some clock that would bring the whole world to a standstill.

I wasn't technically a virgin yet I felt like I was about to give up a different type of innocence to this man, something I would never be able to retrieve.

What if he was aggressive? What would I do? What if he wanted to do something I didn't want to do? Would I have to act, pretending I was having a good time with him? It also crossed my mind that his manhood might be too big for me.

He returned to the room minutes later with a towel wrapped around his waist, and I lay perfectly still while he removed it. He made some comment that I suspected was about my body, but I couldn't understand him. He gently pulled my legs apart and, to my surprise, rather than entering me, he started to rub himself up and down between my thighs until he eventually came to a loud, shuddering climax. I was strangely embarrassed and felt my face flush.

The act had taken no more than ten minutes, and when he was finished he went back into the bathroom to take a shower. I decided to take another shower when he was done. I wanted to wash away all traces of his touch. I scrubbed myself with a bar of soap until my skin was almost raw.

When I was finished, I got dressed, took a deep breath, and opened the bathroom door.

He was sitting on the end of the bed waiting for me. He smiled and thanked me before handing me my fee of 2,000 baht. I *wai*'d in thanks and took the money.

Once I was outside the hotel I counted the money. I had 4,000 baht in total. It would be the equivalent of almost a month's wages if I were working in a factory. I had easily enough money to feed and clothe my family, and perhaps even enough to send something to my mother for Geng.

Knowing the full worth of this sum of money somehow made me feel less guilty about what I'd had to do to earn it. Considering that I didn't have intercourse with him, the situation wasn't nearly as horrific as I'd anticipated. In fact, I surprised myself by hoping that I could find more customers like him. Only hours earlier I'd been in such a state of terror that I thought I might actually be physically incapable of going through with it, and now here I was planning ahead and thinking to myself that maybe this wouldn't be such a bad job after all.

CHAPTER 8

WHEN I ARRIVED at the club for my second night of work, Nhim called me aside. She was pleased that I had returned but she wanted to explain the house rules to me. I had been assigned to the D-unit—a group of go-go dancers who started work at 6pm.

'If you are late, you will be deducted one baht per minute,' she warned me.

It suited me to work nights, because it meant that I would get to spend the day with my children, so I happily agreed.

The 'D-girls', as she liked to call them, were divided into two groups: the casuals and the disciplined. I was to join the latter group, which meant that I wouldn't just use the club to attract clients. I would be paid to dance seven nights a week whether or not I was bought by a client.

The casual girls, I would later discover, turned up whenever they needed money. They were usually more preoccupied with selling themselves to clients rather than encouraging them to spend money in the bar on drinks, as they didn't work on commission. I asked Nhim why she tolerated them.

'The casual girls are usually the youngest and prettiest. They serve as bait with which to lure the customers inside,' she explained.

Nhim was very professional. She was in charge of screening candidates for go-go dancers, supervising staff in her bar, and enforcing the house rules. Her boss decided how much a go-go dancer would be paid on the basis of what she looked like, and how many clients she attracted. The biggest-earning D-girl at the time got 9,000 baht a month.

'It has been decided that you will be paid 7,000 baht a month as well as commission for drinks. You can collect your wage in cash on the second day of every month. The boss will hand the cash to you himself.'

In return, I agreed to work seven nights a week and dance on the stage until the bar closed. Unless, of course, a customer bought me. In that case, the customer would pay me 2,000 baht for a quickie or 4,000 baht for an overnight and pay the bar fine of 500 baht to release me.

Nhim told me that I would have to attend the VD clinic. This was non-negotiable—if I refused I would be fired. To my embarrassment she then called out to one of the other dancers, Chompoo, to arrange the appointment for me.

'Can you show Bua where to get her "oyster" cleaned tomorrow?' she shouted across the bar.

I was shocked by her bluntness. The sight of my mouth falling open caused a ripple of laughter to spread across the room. I had no idea what the procedure involved but I suspected that it had something to do with venereal diseases.

'There is nothing wrong with me. I don't need to be tested,' I said in a low voice.

Nhim took me to one side, away from the titters of the other girls and spoke more discreetly this time, explaining what the procedure would involve.

'Because you go-go girls have sex with men you don't find attractive,' she whispered, 'it is rare for you to become wet or excited. Not to mention that some of you might go out with two or three men a night. This causes friction, which leaves you more open to venereal diseases.

'You are also required to go to the clinic to get your blood tested once every three months. Do you understand?'

She told me that, once a week, a doctor would clean out my vagina for free using a special agent that removes any residue left by the spermicidal lubricants of condoms. If he found any sign of a VD, I would be asked to stop working, and a specialist would give me the correct treatment for it. For the blood test, I had to pay 300 baht and wait a week for the result. I was also given a little book to keep track of my tests.

I turned crimson with embarrassment. Although I was a mother of three children and had made several trips to gynaecologists, I wasn't accustomed to people being so direct about such intimate and personal matters. All I could do was nod my head in silent consent.

Nhim's business acumen and brutal honesty were admirable. She was constantly trying to devise new ways of making money and I secretly wondered if some of her ideas came to her in her sleep, as dreamlike visions.

During my first week working in the bar, Nhim held a meeting where we discussed how to attract more customers into the bar. She held these meetings every three months, and even managed to turn these meetings into a money-making opportunity; any girl who didn't attend the meeting was fined 300 baht for being disrespectful. But Nhim's sense of humour added an element of fun to these meetings and gave us an added incentive to attend, aside from the fear of incurring a fine.

Each meeting began with the usual warning against harassing the customers—which was always a danger when you had so many girls competing together for a man's attention.

'It is no fun for a man to be asked to buy a drink for six girls, one after the other. Spread out,' she would warn.

She would then go on to outline the bar's house rules, as well as identifying any perpetrators from the month gone by. The most common offence was that one or more of the girls had been over-indulging in alcohol. Overeating was another problem, and Nhim warned the girls against getting fat.

'No *farang* wants to watch a dugong dance,' was the common admonition. Nhim took the meetings very seriously; no issue was left uncovered and no topic was considered taboo. We were told that, so long as the client didn't mind, we could have sex during our menstrual cycle.

In order to stimulate more business, Nhim implemented a bonus system. For every five customers a bar girl bagged, she would receive 100 baht as a bonus. Every time I was bought out, I would get a signature on my card so I could keep track of my performance. It wasn't a generous amount, but it was an incentive nonetheless.

As I got to know Nhim better, I began to call her *mae*. Beneath her shrewd businesswoman persona was a softer, more caring side, and she really cared about her dancers. She liked to keep this side of her personality as secretive as possible lest anyone take advantage of it. Nhim gave me some insight into the mind of a client—the various personality types I might encounter and the array of sexual fantasies I might be asked to participate in. She also spent time teaching me how to entice *farang*s to buy drinks at the bar.

On the first trip I made to the VD clinic, there was a group of about ten go-go dancers who hung out on a landing of the building. I quickly became a member of the group, which consisted of women who came from Isan and the north of Thailand. Before work, we did our make-up, ate, and drank while talking comically about experiences we had with customers. I learned a lot of tips and tricks from them about the business.

IT TOOK ME a while to settle into life in the bar. During those first few weeks I would be over-whelmed with apprehension the second a *farang* so much as glanced in my direction. I gradually became more adept at flirting, but when it came to actually propositioning a man, I would freeze up. But I soon mastered the invaluable trick of detaching myself from the event as much as possible. I saw myself as an actress being paid to play a role, and the client was essentially my pay cheque. The other girls used to joke about seeing *farang*s as walking, talking ATM machines. I found it easier to follow suit and standardise the men in such a way, rather than to acknowledge their individual physical features. But every so often a particularly unattractive *farang* would come along and it would take every trick in the book to distance myself.

Nhim told me that fortune had favoured me when I was bought by a *farang* on my first night. Many girls are not so lucky. However, it was several weeks before I met with my next success. In the meantime I danced, flirted, caroused, and did everything I could to hone my talents.

Nhim taught me how to identify which *farang*s were attracted to me based on a split-second glance. She told me to avoid a *farang* wearing sandals and cheap T-shirts no matter how good-looking he is because it means he is probably staying in Khao San Road and won't pay much for the sex. After a lot of practise, I eventually became a master of manipulation—the most lauded talent a prostitute can possess.

TOM WAS THE second *farang* to buy me. He was an older man, with a receding hairline and a rounded paunch that rested on his lap. But with two baht symbols lighting up the pupils of my eyes, I marched over and took a seat beside him.

'Hi, I'm Bua from Khorat,' I said in the friendliest tone I could manage. I gazed into his eyes with what I hoped was a childlike innocence. Young men like you to be flirtatious and outgoing while older men like you to be sweet and demure. His body language was awkward and unsure, and he seemed slightly bewildered by his surroundings. I suspected that this might be his first time in Bangkok and that he had stumbled into the red-light district by accident. Rather than pity his wide-eyed innocence, I immediately recognised what an easy target he would be. I doubted he had any previous experience with go-go girls, so I could charge him as much as I liked and give him as little as possible in return.

I started talking to him in broken English, using my few rehearsed phrases to flatter him and put him at ease; I told him he was very handsome and casually stroked his thigh as I talked. He became very uptight as I touched him, but I pretended not to notice and carried on as normal. He began to relax and before long

I felt his hand creep tentatively along my leg. He started talking more too, spewing forth long and winding sentences that I couldn't understand. I simply nodded in agreement every so often, hoping he wouldn't notice. I must have nodded at an inappropriate juncture though, because he suddenly paused for a few seconds before resuming at a much slower pace.

'I come from America. The USA. You understand?' he said, slowly and deliberately. I simply nodded and started massaging him, hoping to distract him. The conversation continued in this vein for almost an hour until I asked him if he would like to buy some drinks. Guessing that he was a first-timer, I calculated that time and copious amounts of alcohol were the two most crucial ingredients necessary to seduce Tom.

I called a waitress over and ordered two drinks—a bottle of beer for him and a so-called 'lady drink' for me. For every 140 baht he spent on a bottle of beer, I would earn 40 baht. The lady drink was a small glass of cola, which cost 100 baht and I would also get commission from it. I asked him to sign the receipt so I could collect my commission later. So even if we never left the bar, I could still make some money from Tom. The more he drank, the more I flirted, and as Tom got drunker he became much more responsive. Sensing that the timing was right I finally propositioned him.

'You want sex? Or I show you around town?' I asked. He was a little taken aback at first but then nodded in agreement, seemingly unsure of what to do next. I took charge, instructing him that the first thing he needed to do was to pay the bar a release fine. He did as he was told. Even if we never made it out of the bar, the payment ensured that I didn't have to go back on stage and dance half-heartedly for the rest of the night.

If a customer wants to be shown around Bangkok, then the cost of my service is up to him—the average payment is between 1,000 and 2,000 baht. I usually bring them to familiar haunts where the bars remain open until the early hours of the morning. Strictly speaking, these bars are illegal as they are supposed to close at 1 am.

I took hold of Tom's hand and guided him out of the bar. He hadn't specifically asked me to take him to a hotel, so I decided to move on to another bar. As we walked through the streets and lanes of Patpong, he was repeatedly accosted by men waving lists of lewd shows. These take place in clubs located above the bars and are performed by the older women who can no longer attract clients in the go-go bars. Tom was shown pictures of what was on offer, but he seemed more confused by them than anything else; he was probably wondering what role darts and ping-pong balls could possibly have to play in vagina-oriented shows, probably never imagining that women sat on a stage, shooting these items from their vaginas.

The street lights showed Tom to be older than I'd initially thought—his receding salt-and-pepper hairline and his furrowed brow suggested that he was possibly in his fifties. He seemed mesmerised by me. He put his arm around my waist and pulled me closer, with an intimacy that suggested we were girlfriend and boyfriend. The side of his large, protruding belly rubbed against my hip as we walked and he smelled of old, encrusted perspiration, but I didn't resist him. I was a Patpong girl, and my body was all his tonight. I took him to a bar in Pratunam, a favourite hangout of Westerners. We got increasingly drunk until two hours later, Tom finally summoned up the courage to suggest we go back to his hotel room. I told him that my fee for a 'long time' was 6,000 baht, when in fact my usual fee was 4,000 baht. Tom didn't know any better, though, and he eagerly agreed to the figure.

As it turned out, I deserved every extra baht I got because Tom was drunk and barely able to perform. Older men can take a long time to get an erection, and it's hard for them to maintain it. Tom couldn't seem to reach climax through intercourse so I opted to give him a hand job to finish him off. It took me almost two hours to satisfy him. Afterwards, he told me that he intended to stay in Bangkok for the next two weeks and that he would like to see me again. I smiled to myself—some customers seem to feel the need to cover up the fact that they have just paid for sex with the pretence that it was something more meaningful. I was more than happy to see Tom again—so long as he continued to pay me.

I WORKED SEVEN nights a week. The girls at the bar became my closest friends, and my social life began to revolve solely around the red-light district. Patpong became my life and my relationship with Yuth, which was always tenuous, eventually withered and died. We stayed with each other for different reasons; I stayed with him because he took such good care of my children, and he stayed with me because I provided for him and kept him in beer money.

I worked from early evening till the early hours of the morning, and I would be exhausted in the morning when Atid went to school.

Yuth was a completely different person with the children, so I was very relaxed about leaving them in his care. He gladly took Atid to school, bathed them, fetched food and snacks for them, and generally took good care of them, and this was reflected in their behaviour around him.

The change in their attitudes gradually became more noticeable. Peung and Atid no longer cried when I left for work in the evenings, and would occasionally run to Yuth instead of me if they hurt themselves. This upset me greatly, but I comforted myself in the knowledge that at least they were no longer crying themselves to sleep at night from hunger.

I made sure that I still had a large part to play in their lives, and I would play with Peung while we waited for Atid to finish school. As reckless as I have been about my own life, I have never been reckless with my children's lives. Every afternoon before I go to work, I pack Atid's school bag and make sure that he has everything he needs for his education. My children will never know what it's like not to be able to complete an assignment because of lack of money. I also put 500 baht into each of my children's accounts whenever I can spare it. It is done infrequently, and is not much, but it eases my mind knowing that I do something to ensure that they have a better future.

When I worked in Jasmine's I used to feel sorry for the women working in go-go bars. I couldn't comprehend how anyone could bring herself to dance naked in the presence of strangers for the sake of a few baht. I looked down on these girls and considered myself infinitely superior to them. It is a cruel irony that I became everything I once despised. I came to be treated with the same contempt I once doled out to others so freely.

Even the tuk-tuk drivers didn't consider me worthy of their respect. They would shout vulgar comments at me like, 'Oh sister, you have a big guy tonight! I wonder how big he is!'

Oftentimes, if my client happened to be elderly, with white hair and a sagging body, I would walk behind him in order to fool people into thinking we were not together. Despite all the public ridicule I had to contend with, I never became immune to it and there were still moments when all I wanted was to walk through the streets without the title 'bar girl' emblazoned on my forehead in neon letters.

In time I came to learn that this job exposed you to every form of social abuse imaginable. Whereas drugs never appealed to me, many of my friends turned to them to help them cope.

Some girls used ecstasy to get rid of stage fright. I began smoking and drinking heavily. Whether I was dancing at the bar or sleeping with a client, I was usually quite drunk; I found that alcohol helped to anaesthetise me, and after that it was just a matter of going through the motions.

I came to realise that most of the women who worked in these bars had broken spirits. One particularly sad story was that of my friend Parn. She came from the Nakhon Prathom province and had already been working in Patpong for years when I arrived on the scene. She was petite, with short, dark hair, and cheekbones so high that many people mistook her for a ladyboy. Parn lived with her partner in a Klong Toey slum, and they had two sons together, one of whom was crippled. She sent the other son to live with her mother in her hometown. Her story was the same as most of the girls I worked with—she was just trying to get through each night in the bar so that she could earn enough money to support her family.

When I first met her, I found her to be a very sweet girl; she was quite reserved and avoided trouble at all costs. But she started dabbling in amphetamines, and before long I barely recognised her anymore. She and her partner were very vulnerable to the temptation of drugs because they were offered them at every turn in their slum. Both of them began taking amphetamines every day just to cope with life. Each pill cost her 350 baht and she began spending most of her hard-earned money on *yaa baa*—what we Thais refer to as the crazy drug.

Parn couldn't wait to spend her money on the drug, and whenever she couldn't afford to, she would borrow money from other girls. She kept only one or two pills with her in case she was caught by the police. If she carried more on her person, she would be charged as a dealer, not a user. Parn became unbearable. She would often start fights with the other girls over things as mundane as dance moves or make-up. And when she wasn't fighting with someone, she was often to be found passed out at the bar, her head resting on the counter. On one occasion, the *mamasan* caught her flashing her bottom at a couple of men before grabbing one of them by his private parts. Naturally, Nhim cautioned Parn, but rather than apologise for her behaviour, Parn became very irate. She threatened all sorts of violence on Nhim, who was left with no choice but to fire her.

THE POLICE OCCASIONALLY conducted urine tests on the go-go girls but we would usually be warned in advance of their coming. On one occasion, Nhim said any girl who had taken drugs must leave for that night because the police was about to come checking on them. The police didn't come that night, however, I was surprised by the number of girls who left.

A month after the false alarm, a team of police just turned up an hour before the bar was about to close. The officer who seemed to be in charge of the raid told my *mamasan* to stop the music. He told us to line up and other officers handed each of us a lab tube. He then pointed to the toilet where a policewoman was standing next to the door. One by one, we used the toilet and came out with a tube of urine. I handed my tube to an officer and he dropped something in it and I was cleared. I didn't know if they found any drug addicts that night but I saw no arrests.

Drugs were not the only problem that affected the girls of Patpong. On a daily basis, women were being forced to compete with one another to attract men, and this often led to some shocking catfights. I once witnessed a girl get so mad that she hit another girl over the head with a beer bottle. Judging by the amount of blood pouring down the victim's face, I was sure she was dead, but by some miracle she came away needing only four stitches.

Another bloody fight took place outside the bar after closing time one night. It was the climax of a long-time stand-off between two groups of go-go dancers. The leader of one of the groups waited until there were no 'grown-ups' around before producing a razor blade. She attacked one of the opposing group members, cutting a deep gash in her cheek, then sprinted off with her friends. Go-go girls rely chiefly on their looks to attract customers, so the wounded girl was very lucky that she could afford the 100,000 baht needed to pay for the plastic surgery at the reputable Yan Hee Hospital.

Although police maintained a presence in the Patpong area, they rarely investigated reports of such catfights and usually just dismissed them offhand. It would be dishonest of me to give the impression that I never got into a fight myself. In fact, I have been known to start fights on occasion.

Once, a former colleague of mine called On developed a strong dislike for me. I had made some extra money from an especially generous customer and treated a few of my friends and Nhim to grilled chicken. The following night word got back to me that On had been bitching about me to the other dancers, accusing me of throwing money around in an effort to show off. I saw red. I cornered her in the changing room and asked her if the rumours were true. Her cheeks flared up and she denied it, claiming that she had been talking about someone else. A smile played on her lips as she began twirling her hair with her finger in mock innocence. Her defiance incensed me, and I reached out and grabbed her by the hair. Our screams of rage brought the other girls running and it took several of them to pry us apart.

Another time I persuaded a customer to buy me a drink, and we spent some time chatting and getting on well. I knew it was only a matter of time before I could persuade him to pay the bar fine for me, and I excused myself to go to the bathroom. While I was gone, another girl approached him and told him that I had a husband and children at home, that I wasn't fresh anymore, and that he shouldn't waste his money on me.

I had already set the bait and she reeled him in. She stole him from right underneath my nose. In these situations we either talk it out or slap it out.

As I settled into the job, petty jealousies and rivalries consumed me and I thought nothing of fighting like a stray dog to defend my honour. For Thai people, losing face is the greatest source of shame, but as a go-go girl you leave your dignity on the floor of the changing room before you ever take to the stage.

WHILE PROSTITUTION IMPROVED my finances dramatically, it did nothing for my relationship with Yuth, and things continued to deteriorate.

He had temporarily stopped beating me after Peung's birth. For a while, he was so distracted by his little baby girl that he barely seemed to notice me. But when Peung was one year old the beatings resumed.

In the past, Yuth had confined his attacks to behind closed doors, but they gradually became more public. I took his increasing indifference to witnesses as a sign that he had lost all control. The reasons for his attacks hadn't changed; he would regularly accuse me of having affairs with other Thai men if I stayed out too late at night. If I tried to defend myself and argue that I had been servicing a *farang*, he accused me of lying and would proceed to beat me, but if I kept silent it would only confirm his suspicions and he would still beat me. No matter what I did, he beat me.

I often fled to Yuth's mother's house for safety. But Yuth would always turn up the following morning, cradling our daughter in his arms and holding our son's hand, pleading, 'Bua, come home. Don't you love our kids anymore?'

On one occasion, rather than try to defend myself, I just let my body go limp. Seeing that I had no fight in me, Yuth started punching my head repeatedly. For a few seconds everything went black, and then fluorescent spots of yellow started exploding before my eyes like fireworks illuminating a night sky. That was the last thing I remember before I passed out. When I came to, Yuth was sulking in a corner at the opposite side of the room. I think he felt cheated by my blackout because it had prevented him from venting the full force of his violence. My head was throbbing, but I knew why Yuth had concentrated his attack there; he knew better than to hit me where my bruises would be visible because no foreigner would want to purchase a woman covered in ugly black and blue bruises.

As time went by, the beatings got even worse. He stopped caring about the bruises and would just lash out at me wildly, happy to make contact with any part of my body. My screams were his trophies, and the louder they were the more triumphant he felt.

Late one night after work, I was at a roadside eatery with some friends on Surawong Road, which is just beside Patpong, when Yuth called me on my mobile phone, demanding to know where I was. Because he was so far away, I ignored his question and dismissively informed him that I would be home shortly. I should have known better because 30 minutes later he arrived at the food stall. It wouldn't have been too hard to find me, as these stalls catered to all the hungry late-night workers.

He stormed over to me. I could almost smell his anger it was so potent. He reached forward and clasped my throat with his hands. His breath reeked of alcohol.

'You're having an affair! You're running away from me, aren't you?' he screamed at me.

I struggled free of his grasp. The noisy street had come to a standstill and all eyes were on us. I had no face left to lose so I fought back.

'Why would I want to bring more trouble on myself when you are such a bastard to me as it is?'

I had never spoken back to Yuth. He looked momentarily stunned but quickly recovered and began to pummel my face with his fists. I felt like a human punch-bag.

My friends from the bar tried to pull him away, insisting that I had never had an affair.

Yuth finally tired himself out and stopped punching me. I reached my hand up to touch my face, terrified that my features had been reduced to mere pulp. Blood streamed down my face in tear-like rivulets. Yuth couldn't even look at me but instead began to randomly accuse different men of having an affair with me. He even interrogated my friend Off, who was an obviously gay prostitute, but all rationality seemed to have been consumed by sheer jealousy and rage.

Yuth then grabbed me by the arm and dragged me onto the street where he pushed me into a waiting taxi. He continued to punch and slap me for the duration of the journey. I had to use my handbag to deflect his blows from my already mangled face. I tried to make eye contact with the driver in the rear-view mirror, silently beseeching him to intervene, but he just stared resolutely ahead. Even when Yuth threatened to kill me on arrival at our house, the driver still refused to take his eyes off the road. As far as he was concerned, the tearful, bloodied woman in the back of his car was none of his business.

When we reached the shack, Yuth threw 100 baht at the driver and hauled me out of the car. I struggled to break free of him, but I had been greatly weakened by the attack, and Yuth merely laughed at my feeble attempts.

In the shack, Atid and Peung were playing with Yuth's younger sister on the floor. When they heard the door open, they immediately leaped up and ran in my direction, but the sight of my swollen and bloodied face stopped them in their tracks.

Yuth ordered his sister to go home.

Atid instinctively took Peung by the hand and led her upstairs. They both knew all too well what would happen next.

Once they were out of sight, Yuth grabbed me by the throat and repeated his accusations.

'I'm not having an affair, Yuth,' I gasped.

He released his hold only to slap me across the face. Pain seared through my entire body, starting in my face and shooting down to the very tips of my toes. My face was an open wound and this last slap stung more than all of the others throughout the years put together. Yuth's hand came away dripping with blood. He looked down at it in disgust, as if it were excrement. He lent forward and wiped it across my chest, leaving a red smear in his wake.

Yuth warned me one last time not to fuck around on him ever again, or it would be the last time. I knew what he was implying, and I knew what he was capable of. He then turned on his heels and went to bed.

I was in so much pain that my walk had been reduced to a hunched hobble. I edged my way towards the mirror, not quite sure if it was a good idea to look at my reflection, yet needing to confirm that my features were at least all still in the right place, even if they had lost all semblance of their normal selves.

I barely recognised myself. One of my eyes was so swollen as to be practically closed and the white of my other eye had turned a watery red hue. It matched the colour of the rest of my face I thought to myself. My top lip was burst and spewed blood everywhere. My arms were covered in cuts and scratches.

Suddenly, Yuth appeared behind me. He hadn't been able to sleep, so he had come back for a second round. A nightcap, so to speak.

He began kicking and punching me again, this time steering clear of my face—he probably just didn't want to get any more blood on his precious hands.

Despite how badly Yuth had beaten me, I still wanted to go back to work. But Yuth refused to let me leave. He rightly suspected that if I left the house that evening, I might not ever return.

I tried to reason with him that if I didn't go to work then we wouldn't be able to pay the rent. He angrily told me that he would find the money himself, and with that he marched out of the house and slammed the door shut behind him.

I crept upstairs to my children's bedroom and lay down beside them. Darkness protected them from the true horror of my face, but sadly, they had heard my every scream of pain and cry for mercy. Peung asked me what I had done to make her father so angry. I told her I didn't know, but that if she ever found out then maybe she could let me know.

There was still no sign of Yuth the following day when I left the house to go back to the bar. I managed to convince Nhim to let me work as a waitress until the bruises healed. I'm sure she was worried that I might scare the customers away but she felt so sorry for me that she agreed.

A couple of days later Yuth returned home. I was preparing food in the kitchen when he crept up behind me and whispered an apology in my ear.

'I was drunk and got carried away; I don't even remember much of what happened,' he explained.

I kept quiet.

'I'll never do it again. You still love me, don't you?'

Again I didn't say a word. He tried to tickle me but my ribs were so badly bruised that he caused me nothing but pain. I flinched at his touch.

It wasn't just my body that he had beaten to a bloody pulp that night, but also the last vestiges of my love for him.

He handed me a tube of analgesic gel to rub on my bruises. This gesture was intended to be seen as an act of kindness but he was really just trying to cover up his handiwork as fast as possible. I refused to use it as I wanted the rest of the world to witness the full extent of his brutality.

I spent the next few days trying to muster up the courage to leave him.

Phoning the police was never an option as the authorities don't get involved in 'domestic' matters. A husband can even rape his wife without consequence.

Once, when he was sober, I asked him if he ever worried that he might one day hit me so hard that I would be left brain-damaged. He just laughed at the question. He didn't see his actions as having any consequences bar a few cuts and bruises that would eventually fade over time.

CHAPTER 9

THE MAJORITY OF men who frequented the bar were middle-aged and unattractive. But on rare occasions we got a younger, more attractive clientele. I often entertained these men, but I never permitted myself to develop feelings for any of them. Not that these feelings would necessarily have been requited anyway. For a long time I abided by this rule and lived a relatively uncomplicated life—until I met Jack. He was a 35-year-old engineer from California, with short brown hair and blue eyes. He was tall and well-built with a friendly demeanour— I later came to think of him affectionately as a big, friendly giant.

I didn't pay too much attention to him when he first entered the bar. I was busy arguing with a customer who was refusing to pay for drinks, and anyway, one of the other girls had singled him out the second he walked through the door. As my argument with the customer became more heated, I noticed Jack sitting to one side, eavesdropping on the dispute. He appeared to be highly amused by our exchange.

When I first laid eyes on him I immediately questioned what he was doing in the bar—he wasn't the sort of man who needed to pay for the company of a Thai woman.

I eventually called Nhim over to my table to help me deal with the disrespectful customer. The argument escalated even further and, out of the corner of my eye, I could see that Jack was doubled over with laughter. He finally managed to compose himself, and I saw him beckon one of the waitresses over. I overheard him telling her that he would settle the bill.

'It's my lucky day,' I thought to myself as I made my way over to his table. He introduced himself and then offered to buy me a drink.

He spoke slowly so I was able to understand a great deal of what he said. He had a warm and affectionate smile that immediately endeared him to me and made me relax in his company. Unlike most of the *farang*s I had met, Jack seemed to have come to the bar to have fun rather than just to pick up a girl.

The next few hours flew by. I was having such a good time that I forgot that I was supposed to be encouraging Jack to buy drinks, but it didn't matter because he bought numerous rounds anyway.

The night wore on, and eventually, to my dismay, Jack informed me that it was time for him to leave. For the first time since my early days working in the bar, I felt awkward about propositioning a customer. I wasn't sure why, but it somehow felt inappropriate—which is quite ironic considering I am, after all, a go-go girl.

I asked him to come back again soon and then *wai*'d him goodbye. But to my surprise, he asked if I would like to accompany him to another bar. I delightedly accepted the offer but told him that he would have to pay the bar the standard fine to enable me to leave. He seemed unperturbed and handed the money over to Nhim as I got changed into more suitable clothes. We left the bar hand in hand. From the beginning, I felt more like his date rather than a prostitute.

Although Jack wasn't drunk, he was definitely merry. He decided to meet up with a friend in Nana, which is another red-light area similar to Patpong and Soi Cowboy. I had never been there but heard from my colleagues that Nana girls asked for about 1,500 baht for a quickie, and the competition among them was even worse than among the Patpong girls.

Jack waved down a taxi, and when we climbed in, the taxi driver tried to rip him off by charging 200 baht for a trip to Nana. He refused to pay the fare, pointing in the direction of the BTS SkyTrain track overhead, and waved the driver off. It was evident that he knew a lot about Bangkok, which made me curious—I had never met a *farang* before who knew his way around so well.

The train journey to Nana took less than 20 minutes. When we got off at our stop, we walked the few minutes journey to Sukhumvit Soi 4, passing bars and street vendors selling deep-fried insects. The next thing I saw was the Nana Plaza, a three-storey sex-entertainment mall. It consisted of go-go bars and beer bars; there were also ladyboy go-go bars, which were overflowing with *farang*s.

We met Jack's friend in a go-go bar on the second floor. The clientele seemed to be a mixture of *farang*s and Japanese tourists. Jack's friend had already bought one of the girls, so the four of us left to have a drink elsewhere. As we walked, Jack told me a little bit about himself. My English was still very bad, but I managed to piece together several bits of information. I learned that he worked for a phone company and regularly travelled between Thailand, Germany and China. I was surprised to hear that he had been single for a long time, but I figured it must be difficult to hold down a relationship when he was away travelling so frequently.

At the end of the night Jack took out his wallet and counted out 4,000 baht. He pressed the notes into my hand and, staring deep into my eyes, asked me if I would like to spend the night with him at his hotel in Klong San. I knew Jack was supposed to be just another client, but somehow this transaction felt a lot more personal.

I was relieved to discover that he didn't have any kinky fetishes; all he wanted was straightforward sex. Jack was also the first *farang* to make me climax.

I SPENT THE next seven days and nights with Jack. He would pay my release fine and we would then explore the nooks and crannies of Bangkok before falling into bed in his hotel room in the early hours of the morning. His interest in me wasn't purely sexual, though. He took me shopping on a few occasions and would always insist on holding my hand, clutching onto me tightly as if I were his most treasured possession. He took me to his favourite restaurant, the Hard

Rock Café in Siam Square, and lavished gifts on me. Customers dining at neighbouring tables seemed more interested in the teddy bear and flowers adorning my table than the food sitting in front of them. We attracted puzzled stares wherever we went, with people keen to figure out the exact nature of our relationship—was I just another bar girl, or did I mean something more to him? The public speculation didn't bother me though; I felt like Jack's *jao yhing*; his princess, and from high up on my pedestal the rest of the world was just a collection of meaningless small black dots. All I could see was Jack.

Our courtship, if I can call it that, was exhilarating, but when Jack asked me if I had any children, reality stepped in. I was terrified that I was about to wake up from this wonderful daydream we had both been sharing, so I lied to him—something I had become very adept at over the last few years. I told him that I was single and had just recently started working in the bar.

Occasionally a client would notice the scar I had on my stomach from my sterilisation operation. I decided to go for a permanent sterilisation after the birth of Peung because I realised that I couldn't cope with any more children. When a client commented on my scar, I would cover up by only telling part of the truth: that I had children to feed after I broke up with my abusive husband. I would tell this story if I thought it would generate sympathy. Other times I would tell them I had an operation and would leave it at that. To tell a client that I was still with Yuth would be a big turn-off for them.

I like to think that I lied to Jack as much for his sake as my own. No bar girl will ever admit to having a partner or being a mother—and truth be told, no *farang* really wants to hear the truth. They have paid for the privilege of enacting their fantasy, and an exotic young nymphomaniac fits the bill much better than a financially destitute mother of three.

When his visit to Thailand came to an end, Jack asked me if I would like to stay in touch with him. On the one hand, I was scared of letting myself become too attached, but on the other, I knew that Jack had stopped being just a customer to me. And so I agreed. He set up an email account for me and, because I had never used a computer before, he brought me to an internet café to show me what to do.

On the day of Jack's departure, my sister accompanied us to Don Muang Airport. Her English was far superior to mine and, not knowing when I would see Jack again, I wanted her to help me communicate to him the flurry of emotions he had given rise to. Needless to say, I had made it clear to Jack that my sister didn't know I worked as a bar girl, and I didn't want her to find out.

When the time came to say goodbye, Jack embraced me tightly, nestling his head against my shoulder. Jack was on the verge of tears and, despite my own intense sadness, I found myself soothing him and reassuring him that we would be reunited soon. For a second I let myself forget about Yuth, Atid, Peung, and Geng. I wasn't a bar girl and Jack wasn't my client; we were boyfriend and girlfriend being torn apart by a temporary business trip. But the final boarding call jolted me out of my reverie. Jack reluctantly pulled away. He kissed me goodbye one last time before he disappeared into the crowds.

My sister promised that she would help me translate Jack's emails and compose a reply. Both she and *mae* knew about our relationship and they saw Jack as my *farang* in shining armour, come to whisk me away to a better life.

I WAS STILL very emotional when I presented myself for work that evening. Nhim noticed the dramatic change in my mood.

'Is there something wrong? Has your *farang* gone home?' she asked.

I nodded. Nhim had very little patience for girls who developed feelings for their customers. She had warned us time and time again that we were only setting ourselves up for heartbreak.

'You may as well forget him because he has already forgotten you,' she chastised me.

Fearing there might be some truth in what she said, I checked my email account as soon as I got the chance. To my relief I had received an email from Jack. He had written it only hours after we said goodbye at the airport.

Dear Bua,

I arrived home 15 minutes ago. Such a long trip and it is pouring down with rain here. It was very sad having to leave you at the airport and I thought about you the whole way home. I will always remember the time that we spent together. I hope very much that you will keep in touch with me and I will see you very soon again. I wish I could look into your eyes again right now, they are just so beautiful. I miss you a lot. You are such a sweet, kind and happy lady with a cute smiling face that I will never forget – even if I have lost most of the pictures I took of you because my stupid phone died :(

Shy, innocent but sexy is such a powerful combination. You really got into my heart so quick and it was easy to fall in love with you.

I had such a good time with you every night – the week went so quick. You and your sister took me to some great places where I really had a great time. Parting is such sweet sorrow and I really had to fight hard to keep from crying at the airport. It was soooooooooo hard to actually go through the door and not be able to see you anymore.

That woman I ran into at the airport just as I was about to leave was one of my former co-workers from my last job. She teased me a lot in the immigration line. I got totally caught up with you at the very last minute! But I don't care anymore.

Something funny happened to my watch. The whole trip from Bangkok to California I could not change the time so my watch was stuck on Bangkok time like it was telling me that I should not have left you, I should have stayed. Not until after I landed in California was I finally able to change the time. It was very weird as I had tried many times throughout my journey. I thought my watch had broken as well as my phone. So the whole trip home I knew exactly what time it was in Bangkok and kept thinking about what you might be doing right then. I expect you are still asleep now as it's 7am in Bangkok.

Something else that is funny is that I think I left my aftershave lotion (perfume) in the bathroom. Maybe the hotel still has it. If they have it maybe I can get them to keep it for you at reception for a few days and you could get it and keep it as a memory of me. Maybe put some on the teddy bear I bought you so that he smells like me. Would you like me to ask the hotel to keep it for you if they have it? I think I will need your last name for them to hold it for you. What is your last (family) name?

Say hi to your sister for me (if she is not helping you read this). It was very nice of her to come all the way to the airport for us.

Well I have to go now and wash a lot of clothes. I have to leave again on Tuesday and will be really busy tomorrow. I hope that by tomorrow morning I will have an email from you even if it just says 'Hi, I got your mail.' I would rather have a small email from you soon than have to wait a while for you to write a long one that I know will be hard for you.

So write me soon and please stay SAFE.

Love, hugs and kisses
Jack

The sentiments Jack expressed in his email quelled any lingering doubts that he was interested only in my body. I felt reassured that he was as emotionally involved in our relationship as I was.

Thai women tend to evaluate a relationship first and foremost in terms of a man's potential to provide them with a proper home and income. Jack ticked both these boxes, and I let myself believe that one day an email would arrive telling me that he had booked me onto the next flight to California. Surely it was only a matter of time. Aside from financial security, though, I also believed that Jack could offer me something else that no amount of money could buy—and that was love.

Jack returned to Thailand a month later and we took up where we'd left off. I couldn't afford to quit working in the bar as I still needed an income to support Yuth and our children, so I insisted that Jack pay for my time. So each night I would take to the stage in my bikini top and thong and Jack, for his part, would play the role of the customer. He would gallantly pay my release fine and whisk me away from the bar. But the novelty factor of our act soon began to wear off, and I yearned for a normal relationship. In the beginning I thought of Jack as my saviour and truly believed that he would rescue me from the bar in Patpong. But as time wore on, it began to worry me that Jack was more than willing to continue our charade in the bar. I tried to convince myself that this meant nothing and that his love for me was sincere.

During Jack's second visit, he asked me if he could meet my mother. In Thailand, such an introduction marks a significant turning point in a relationship. At the time, *mae* was living with Geng in the Rangsit district of Bangkok. I used to visit them both most weekends, enjoying seeing my three children play together.

My family were still unaware that I was working as a go-go dancer and were instead under the impression that I had a job as a waitress in a busy restaurant that catered for foreigners. I told my mother that Jack had been a regular customer of mine that I had gradually gotten to know while serving him. Strictly speaking, my story wasn't wholly untrue. I'm not sure whether or not my mother actually believed me though. I think that even if she did suspect the truth, she refused to acknowledge it and was much happier to go along with the version of events that I offered her.

Mae welcomed Jack with open arms. She saw him as the antithesis of Yuth, whom she had gradually come to hate. She gave Yuth the nickname *san lang yao*, meaning 'very lazy', or when she was feeling especially vindictive she would call him *ga fak*, after a species of parasite plant. She pinned all her hopes for my happiness on Jack and saw him as my only chance of escaping from the clutches of poverty.

ALTHOUGH JACK WAS very popular with the other girls in the bar, Nhim didn't like him. She never openly voiced her reservations about him but instead disguised them in thinly veiled comments advising me against getting too attached to him. She saw him as just another *farang* and believed that if you scratched away the surface, his sweet words would give way to the usual lies and broken promises. I took no notice of Nhim though. I saw him as the first man in my life who didn't try to control me. I interpreted how comfortable he was with my job as a good thing—I took it as a sign that he wasn't the jealous, possessive type. In my eyes he was everything that Chai and Yuth weren't.

His wealth and generosity also attracted me. He reminded me of Hiroshi in that respect. He thought nothing of buying me expensive gifts or taking me on extravagant shopping trips. I had lived all my life in such an extreme state of poverty that I was dazzled by Jack's wealth and the nonchalance with which he spent it. For his part, I think he appreciated the fact that I didn't give him a hard time when other girls flirted with him at the bar. I pretended not to be jealous, even going so far as to tell him that he was welcome to have fun with other girls if he wanted. But I was secretly terrified that there would come a night when he would pay the release fine for another girl and bring her back to his hotel room instead of me. I needn't have worried, though, because Jack only had eyes for me.

I was also impressed by his fun-loving nature. He sometimes went up to the stage and danced with the girls, making people laugh at him. Despite her scepticism, Nhim didn't try to stop him because he was a good customer who generously bought lots of drinks. After Jack's debut on stage, Nhim even teased him back onto the stage again. By then, all the staff knew who he was and why he was there. The girls constantly told me how lucky I was to have met him.

Over the next few months our relationship developed into something of a routine. On arrival in Bangkok, Jack would ring and ask me to come to his hotel at once. Unaware that I had a partner and two children at home, he wouldn't expect me to have any prior commitments. If I was with Peung and Atid I would try to come up with some excuse, but in Jack's eagerness to see me, he would insist that any other arrangements I had should be secondary to seeing him. I found it increasingly difficult to juggle my two different lives and worried that it was only a matter of time before they collided.

He began to tell me that he loved me and held my hand wherever we went. I never told him that I loved him back; instead I tried to look happy.

As time passed, I began to gradually distance myself from Jack. I did this to protect myself because I knew we had no future together.

I had long since fallen out of love with Yuth, but leaving him would have meant leaving our children because the more time I spent with Jack the more I realised he would never accept them. In that respect he was like every other *farang* I had ever slept with—keen to gloss over the fact that he was far from the first man I'd had scx with. Such baggage would have stifled Jack's free-spiritedness, and I knew that such a revelation would potentially shatter our relationship. I gradually began to realise that Jack was in love with a woman who didn't exist, and it became a daily struggle to maintain this illusion and prevent him from discovering the real me.

Once I spotted the first crack in our relationship, it wasn't long before the entire structure began to give way. I became increasingly disappointed with Jack's indifference to my working in the bar. He must have known that I was sleeping with other men while he was away, and if he truly loved me then surely this prospect should have repulsed him. He was wealthy enough to have been able to subsidise my income in the bar and allow me to stop working. But he never once suggested this. I began to suspect that his feelings for me stemmed from an infatuation rather than true love. I began to feel like a mere plaything, to be taken out and enjoyed whenever he felt like it. I think he came to like being in control. When he was in Bangkok, he wanted me constantly by his side. I would make up excuses in order to spend a day with Atid and Peung. Other times I would bring friends with me when he asked me to meet him alone. It meant I wasn't 'on' all the time, struggling to talk and listen to English, or struggling to be something I wasn't.

I often wondered whether things might have been different if I had been more honest with him from the beginning, but I very much doubted so. If Jack had wanted a normal, committed relationship with me, then his impression that I had no familial ties should have encouraged him to suggest I move back to America with him. This realisation tainted my feelings for him.

Every time I accompanied Jack to Don Muang Airport to see him off, he would weep uncontrollably. Perhaps in some countries it is acceptable to see a grown man cry, but in

Thailand it is seen as extremely emasculating. My embarrassment at Jack's open display of emotion was only compounded by the fact that as my feelings for him began to lessen, so too did my displays of emotion in the departure lounge. On one occasion, I rubbed *ya mhong*, a menthol-based balm, into my eyes to make them water. The sight of my teary eyes only served to heighten Jack's emotions, so from then on, I thought it was safer to be dry-eyed than to risk Jack bawling like a newborn baby.

Even though Jack had the role of a love-struck man down to a tee, his performance stopped ringing true. He sent me emails from all over the world telling me how desperately he missed me and how he couldn't stop thinking about me, yet I began to sense that there was something insincere about his sentiments.

When he was away from Bangkok he emailed me regularly, and if I didn't reply immediately he would send a series of new emails pretending to be gravely worried about my lack of response. Once again I questioned myself why, if he was so concerned about my well-being, he didn't help me escape from Patpong.

His emails became increasingly frequent and I realised that yet again I had sorely misjudged a man. He was indeed the possessive type. Throughout our relationship, not one night

had passed where Jack had neglected to pay
me for my time. Even when the relationship
escalated and things had clearly progressed past
a professional point, he still insisted on paying
me. I think he secretly enjoyed the sense of
ownership these payments bought him. Whereas
Chai and Yuth had used their fists to keep me in
line, Jack used money and words. Jack's emails
were like beautiful silken cobwebs, laced with
poetic declarations whose sole intention was to
ensnare me in a sticky residue of guilt.

Hi Bua darling,
I leave China tomorrow and have to move further
away from you for a while. But you are always close
in my heart. I miss you soooooooooooooooooooooooo
much. Every night is lonely without you. I look at
your photograph often and wish I was with you.
I checked my email often but nothing from you
yet :(
I have not had an email from you for about a
week so I am getting worried again. I hope you
are OK. Please write soon as your emails make me
happy. I sad now :(
You are in my dreams every night. I cuddle my
pillow instead of you but it is not the same. I need
you with me.

I hope you are still hugging the bear I bought you – he is a lucky bear if you are. I hope he keeps you with warm thoughts of me.

Write soon please! I check my email every day to see if you have written.

I love you with all my heart darling. Please wait for me also, don't forget about me.

All my love, hugs and kisses
Jack

As time passed, I came to resent him. I hated him for being possessive. I didn't like the way he sent email after email demanding that I answer him.

I often tried to write to him using lovers' language but such sentiments were new to me and I didn't find them natural to convey in writing.

I could not however ignore the money that he provided. *Mae* had often asked about Jack and warned me to stay in contact with him.

Although my feelings for him had completely changed, I felt trapped by the money I stood to lose if I ended our relationship. With so much competition from the other girls in the bar, it wasn't always easy to attract a *farang*, but when Jack was visiting Bangkok I didn't have to worry about this.

There were many nights when no one bought me out, and I would have to rely solely on the commission I earned from drinks I might sell. And so, long after the initial flush of love had faded away, I continued on in the relationship.

The fact that my English was so terrible, coupled with my waning feelings for Jack, made it increasingly difficult to reply to his emails, even with my sister's help. It was for this reason that I befriended a man who worked in an internet café in Soi Patpong 2. He was fluent in English, and for a fee of 50 baht he agreed to translate my emails for me. I considered the fee a paltry amount given all the money Jack had paid me over the months. The arrangement would also be a worthwhile investment if it helped me to retain Jack's patronage.

Almost a year to the day we first met, I received a strange email. I scanned over the content and saw that although Jack's name was mentioned several times he did not appear to be the sender. I called my friend in the internet café over to help me decipher it. He read through it quickly.

'There is trouble with Mr Jack,' he said.

I looked at him quizzically.

'You listen. I read. But you're not going to like this,' he warned.

The email was from a girl called Sarah, claiming to be Jack's fiancée. She wanted to know if I was the girl he'd been buying gifts for while visiting Thailand. She also wanted to know if I would meet her in person. She ended the email with a curt comment about hoping that I would at least have the decency to reply to her.

I was completely stunned. My translator sat beside me, trying to hide his smile. He had been following our relationship for some time now through the various emails he had translated, and he clearly found this new development amusing. I think that, like Nhim, he had seen this coming all along and thought me a fool for thinking Jack would be any different to other *farang*s. At first I couldn't help but feel grossly deceived by him but then it hit me that I was guilty of exactly the same deception.

I decided against replying to Sarah. She seemed to be looking for answers, and I didn't feel that I had any to give her—that was Jack's responsibility. I decided instead to send Jack an email, simply asking him who Sarah was and that she had written to me requesting I meet her. I knew that such an email would mark the end of our relationship and, more importantly, my income from Jack, but I suspected that Sarah's discovery of our affair had already sounded the death knell anyway. Jack never responded.

I sent him another nine emails looking for an explanation, but he didn't reply to any of them. My mother and sister were more upset by our break-up than I was. All of their hopes for my happiness sailed off into the sunset with Jack. But for me, the honeymoon period had ended long ago, and Jack's wallet was the only thing about him that I still found remotely attractive.

The relationship was a lie from beginning to end. I often think of him and wonder if he did marry Sarah, or if she cancelled her wedding.

Did I hate him afterwards? Yes and no. I didn't hate him because he had a girlfriend; I hated him because he lied. Then I reminded myself that I was also a liar.

His initial sheen had worn off, and he had slowly become more and more transparent. It had taken me some time to fully accept it, but Jack had never had any intention of gallantly sweeping in on horseback and rescuing me from my life. I was just a playmate for him when he was away from his fiancée. I had been forced to compete with many other girls over the years in the bar, but I had also learned to recognise when I was no match for my opponent. And in this case, Jack's fiancée was always going to be the victor.

CHAPTER 10

CONTRARY TO WHAT our customers would like to believe, bar girls do not enjoy selling their bodies. We fake moaning and feign enjoyment to arouse the men further, hoping they will ejaculate quickly. We don't want to spend one more minute with them after they climax, unless they pay us extra. I personally don't like to be cuddled in the wet and sticky embrace of an older man.

Of course it eases the unpleasantness somewhat if the customer is not fat, does not smell like a pot-bellied pig, and is easy on the eye. But offering your body up to strangers to use and abuse as they see fit is not a vocation any woman chooses, but rather is one born of desperation.

It is for this reason that few bar girls will ever admit to what we do for a living. Instead, we spin elaborate lies and concoct intricate stories to conceal the truth. The only person who knew what I did for a living was Yuth. I dared not tell my parents or my sister because I was afraid of losing face or humiliating them. But I suspected that they knew the truth. They must have wondered how I managed to earn enough money from waitressing to support my children and an unemployed husband.

Whenever I felt like running away, I thought of my children. I had become a prostitute solely to give them a better childhood than the one I'd had. A job in a factory would barely have put enough food on the table for one person, never mind a family of four. It was never a simple matter of walking away from Patpong. Initially, this way of life and the money I earned from it had been a crutch, helping me to walk again after the crippling effects of poverty. But somewhere along the way this crutch had become the very backbone of my existence; its vertebrae like tendrils wrapping themselves around my every organ. I was trapped.

Almost all of the girls I worked with in the bar found it difficult to cope on a day-to-day basis. For me, alcohol possessed palliative powers, whilst other girls found comfort in drugs. But there were some for whom no amount of drink, drugs, or money helped ease their pain. Some of these girls fell prey to depression, and I watched them retreat further and further into themselves, powerless to help them.

One such girl was my friend Priew. By the time Priew started working in the bar I had already been there for a year. She was a tall, strikingly beautiful girl from the north of Thailand. Girls from the north are known for their fair complexion and sweet manner. She never told anyone what province she was from for fear that word of her new profession would make its way back to her family and friends.

When Priew first started working in the bar, Nhim decided that she should work as a casual girl because *farang*s were clearly transfixed by her. Men flocked around her, driving the other girls in the bar crazy with jealousy. She just danced and waited to be chosen. Sometimes two men wanted to buy her at the same time. My first impression of Priew was that she was arrogant, as she didn't mix with the other girls at all. I would often say hello to her when I arrived for my shift in the bar, but she would just stare mutely into space, refusing to acknowledge my greeting. It was only as I got to know her better that I realised her isolation wasn't self-inflicted, but rather the result of the other girls' efforts to punish her for her beauty. One of the few things that made working in the bar a little more bearable was the camaraderie that usually existed between us girls: the fact that Priew was being excluded from this must have made her life that little bit more miserable.

I found her crying in the toilet one night just before closing time. Her only defence against the other girls had been the mask of indifference she had so carefully applied. But as she stood before me now, with mascara-laden tears streaming down her cheeks, I realised that beneath her glacial exterior lay a very sad and troubled girl.

I asked her what was wrong, tentatively placing my arm around her in an effort to comfort her.

'I can't live like this anymore. What if my parents see me like this? I hate myself for what I have become,' she blubbered.

Priew went on to explain how she had first come to be a go-go dancer in Patpong. She told me that several years ago her partner had accumulated huge gambling debts that they were unable to repay. Not knowing what to do, she turned to her sister for advice. Her sister was a go-go dancer in Patpong and told her that she could spend the rest of her life trying to repay the debt on a meagre factory wage, or she could make more money than she could ever imagine working in the bars of Patpong. Priew reluctantly agreed to the proposition. But it came to be, she said, the biggest mistake of her life.

She told me about the first time she had been bought by a *farang*. Like me, she was bought on her first night in the bar. It can be bad for confidence levels to have to struggle for weeks on end to attract a *farang,* but at the same time, for a terrified newcomer, it is potentially very damaging to have to sleep with a stranger on your very first night.

The *farang*, she said, had been a much older man. He took her back to his hotel room and asked her to remove her clothes. When she broke down in tears he told her he didn't mind waiting until the following morning if she would feel more comfortable about sleeping with him then. He even paid her 4,000 baht upfront in an effort to get her to relax. But as soon as the *farang* fell asleep, Priew got dressed and fled the hotel.

Her beauty secured her a second customer the following night. He was a shy, well-dressed Chinese man. For 2,000 baht, she agreed to accompany him to his hotel. Once there, they sat on the bed and began making awkward small talk. The night wore on, and the Chinese man still hadn't made an advance. Priew began to wonder if he had paid her simply for her company. Or was he perhaps expecting her to be the aggressor? But after several hours, and numerous lengthy silences, he finally seemed ready to make a move. He began to unbutton his shirt, and in a hushed, embarrassed-sounding tone, he said that he hoped she would be able to cope with his condition. Not knowing what he was referring to, and feeling increasingly panicky with every button he undid, Priew simply nodded in reply. But she gasped in horror when he took off his shirt and revealed the nature of his 'condition'.

His upper body was covered in long, purple, welt-like scars and he wore a prosthetic leg. His good leg had been harvested for skin grafting. Only his neck and lower arms had been spared. He looked like he had been whipped to within an inch of his life. Priew couldn't take her eyes off him, and it was only when he pulled his shirt back on that she finally looked away. The Chinese man didn't say anything, just lowered his head in a resigned manner as if to say that this was exactly the reaction he had been anticipating. It was at that moment that Priew stopped being scared of sleeping with him. She realised that the money this man was offering her in exchange for sex not only bought him the right to her body but also her indifference to his bodily defects. The Chinese man was to be the first of many customers that Priew slept with.

Whereas she learned not to judge customers, be it on their looks or personality, she became highly critical of herself. Her self-respect dwindled with every customer she slept with.

Priew finished her story and continued sobbing in my arms for some time afterwards. Like so many other girls I knew, the sex industry had chewed her up and spat her out. She was a broken woman; the remnants of her self-esteem lay shattered on the ground, like miscellaneous pieces of a jigsaw puzzle that no longer made up a complete picture. I helped her get up and asked if she wanted to go for something to eat with me and some friends. She instantly agreed, and from that moment on she became like my little sister.

I OFTEN WONDERED if the *farang*s who frequented Patpong ever stopped to ask themselves why we chose this life. Did they recognise our desperation, and realise that we sold our bodies purely as a means of survival? Did they ever wonder about the lives we led outside of the bars and their hotel rooms?

Patpong girls slowly become mere shadows of their former selves. If we didn't become hardened to the job we do, then we couldn't cope with the emotional toll we inflict on ourselves. We have learned to make light of our situation and laugh about it although we are dying inside.

Priew never showed any sign of weakness to me again. She drank and smoked regularly and became business-like, with her eyes fixated on the money she would made.

These days she talks to me about how expensive oil is and about the insurance premium for her car, all the while trying to cover up the fact that she was the woman who once broke down in my arms. I guess she had to harden herself and conceal her despair in order to survive in Patpong.

She and her sister had been sending money back to their mother at home. Like me, Priew's father had a *mia noi* but she talked openly about how she came to despise her *por* because he slapped her sister in the face after she had a fight with the *mia noi*. Her father later broke up with his second wife and reconciled with their mother after he found out that his daughters had been supporting her.

My close friends and I made a pact that we would try to help each other get through the night more easily, whenever it was possible. Whenever one of us succeeded in securing a customer, she would ask him if he wanted service from her friend as well. A client could buy as many girls as he liked, and I was more comfortable being bought out along with my close friends. One of us would give oral sex while the others would caress his body. For couples who had bought us, we would put on a lesbian show while they had sex. Competition and jealousy were already high in the bar and at the end of the day we just wanted to make as much money as we could. We found it was more productive to work together rather than prey on the same target.

Priew and I were bought by two young white men once. We went into separate rooms. An hour later, I finished my job and was waiting for her to come out. I knocked on her door, and Priew said she would be with me in ten minutes. When we met up at the lobby I asked her why it took her so long. She almost burst out laughing as she told me that, for the first time, she had met a man with a downturned erect penis. She compared it to an upside down tusk of an elephant. It was difficult for them to figure out a way to have intercourse. She said they changed from one position to another, but his penis kept sliding out. He had never been with a woman before because he had been so embarrassed about the shape of his penis, and he couldn't figure out the best way to have intercourse when he was with Priew.

He couldn't ejaculate, even when Priew gave him a hand job and a blow job. They both became resigned to the fact that he wouldn't orgasm, but the man gave her 2000 baht for her time.

Another friend of mine, Roj, first started working as a prostitute when she was 17 years old. I met her when she was 30, and by that time she had slept with hundreds of *farang*s. Like me, she gave up school because her family was poor.

She often reminisced about her early days as a prostitute, which she claimed had been a lot simpler. At first I found it difficult to equate this nostalgia with such a cold and degrading industry, but Roj described what it had once been like. She claimed that when she had first started out, customers had been a lot less demanding and a lot more generous—a winning combination. The advent of the internet and the increase in foreign travel meant that *farang*s began exchanging tips and offering one another advice. The balance of power shifted as the men became more savvy.

Roj enjoyed the support of many *farang* patrons during her early years, allowing her to take extended breaks from the industry. Inevitably, however, these patrons drifted back to their wives, and Roj returned to work in the bar. But she never begrudged these men and seemed to accept their wives' precedence as only fair and natural. Roj understood that we girls would never be anything more than fleeting fancies to *farang*s.

I came to love Roj as if we were family, and I affectionately called her my sister. We never competed with one another for customers but often teamed up when approaching a *farang*, claiming to be sisters. Oftentimes, if one of us grew tired of trying to satisfy a customer, the other would change the condom and take over. But we always divided the fee, regardless of whether or not we had both slept with the customer.

Once we double-dated two men, one of whom was severely scarred on the face. We agreed to go out with them because they were very generous with money. Roj bravely volunteered to sleep with the scarred man and assigned me to deal with the other one. Once we were in their hotel room, the other man and I excused ourselves into the bathroom to do our business, leaving Roj and Scar Face in the bedroom. After we finished we were paid handsomely—6,000 baht for less than two hours' work. Roj showed her callous side by telling me what had happened between her and Scar Face. She told me she was on top of him, swaying her head all the time, pretending to enjoy the sex. She did it so her hair would cover her eyes, thus preventing her from the sight of his damaged face. If he were on top of her she couldn't avoid seeing his face. She joked that all the time she kept thinking about the money, and wondered how long it would take him to climax. After she finished, I was about to hand her an extra 1,000 baht for taking the harder job, but she insisted we share the fee equally as always.

Roj gave me a lot of invaluable advice. She helped me to tailor my behaviour to suit the different classifications of clients I would be dealing with. She told me that the older *farang*s preferred the more ladylike girls; the middle-aged men were attracted to gentler girls; and the younger men liked flirty, outgoing girls.

Roj openly admitted to the fact that the industry had hardened her.

'*Farang*s use us so why shouldn't we use them in return,' I often heard her say, without a trace of emotion. She was one of the few prostitutes I knew who didn't let herself be defined by what she did. She was also the only girl I met who thought that the increase in Thai women entering prostitution was a result of Thai society being more open about our kind of women. I didn't agree with this sentiment, though. I saw no evidence that people were more accepting of prostitutes, and I still felt too ashamed to tell anyone what I worked at.

To Roj, sex was just a product to be sold to the highest bidder; she saw *farang*s as fools, with more money than sense, willing to part with their cash for a few moments of pleasure. And if Roj could exploit this weakness and make a living from it, then all the better for her.

Roj had countless stories about the strange men she encountered. But one story in particular both amused and terrified me so much that I would regularly ask her to recount it; each time she would add a new colourful detail that would have me squealing in delight.

Roj accompanied a *farang* back to his hotel room one night. The client in question was a small wiry man with a furrowed brow that gave him an anxious expression. His voice was a low, almost inaudible squeak, not unlike a mouse Roj had said. He wrung his hands nervously during the taxi ride and seemed to be of a timid disposition. However, as soon as they reached his hotel room all this changed. He produced a leather whip from the wardrobe, and the little mouse that had paid for Roj's company vanished into thin air. In his place was a much more confident man, who cracked the whip against the bed with an evil glint in his eye. Just as Roj was about to run out the door, he reassured her that he had no desire to hurt her but instead wanted her to be the one administering pain. He stripped off and requested that she put her full force into the lashes. He even demonstrated what he meant by striking the whip against the bed several times before lying facedown on the bed. Roj cracked the whip above him, trying not to let the smile playing on her lips undermine her dominatrix act.

As she was nearing the end of the session she accidentally whipped herself, producing a long purple welt on her arm. She had to buy cooling gel and plasters on her way home to try to conceal what had taken place that night.

Roj was completely mystified by how anyone could achieve sexual gratification from such a violent act. I had no answer for her. Despite the many years that we had both worked in prostitution, neither of us had come across this particular fetish before, although I now realise that it is not uncommon.

I sometimes feel that I have been protected, in many ways, from the really horrible side of prostitution. I haven't had too many bad experiences, relatively speaking, and I try to learn from my friends.

We always have a shower when we go back to the client's hotel, and we insist that the man shower too because hygiene is an extremely important part of our job. One night when Roj stepped out of the shower in a *farang's* hotel room, she decided to skip the small talk and get straight down to business. He was sitting on the bed with a towel around him, waiting for Roj to take the lead. She adopted her most seductive expression and whipped his towel from him. Although he had already showered, she was greeted by the most pungent smell from his penis. She said it appeared that he hadn't cleaned his shaft since his last life, as he had quite a lengthy foreskin, and he obviously didn't bother washing underneath it. She immediately gagged, so overwhelming was the smell. It was apparent that he wanted a blow job, but Roj told him that he'd have to wear a condom while she smoked him.

He refused, and was quite crude to her, saying that if she insisted on blowing him with a condom, he'd rather bang her. He finally agreed to pay 1,500 for a blow job with a condom. He spoke Thai quite fluently, and told her that he was a good lover. He then sneakily added that he'd pay her 2,000 baht if she agreed to smoke him raw.

'Not in this life,' she retorted. Roj said that she grabbed a towel and started to rub his penis in an attempt to clean it somewhat, and remove the mucus and encrusted dirt.

'Do I disgust you?' he asked, almost appearing amused by this turn of events.

'I use my mouth to eat, not to perform this type of job.'

'Very well, if it's such a big deal, I'll just bang you then.'

Roj jumped back onto the bed where he proceeded to suck on her nipples. She always cringed and laughed as she recounted this part of the tale, almost as if it was worse than the smelly penis. He sucked her breast as if he was trying to breast-feed, sucking even harder than her children had while she was nursing them. It was unfortunate for Roj that she was quite sober at the time because it started to hurt her, especially when he entered her and kept on pumping at her until her inner thighs grew sore. Although she asked him to climax quickly, it went on for some time until Roj could take no more. She asked him to stop, and just to pay her 1,000 baht and she would leave immediately. They had been having sex for almost an hour at this point, and Roj suspected that he had taken Viagra. He eventually removed himself from her and started to jerk off in front of her face. Roj kept her lips firmly together, but he managed to grab her head with his free hand and used his fingers to pry her mouth open. Roj kept her mind on the money, and as soon as he ejaculated, she ran back into the shower, and then grabbed her things ready to go.

'What's your hurry?' the *farang* drawled.

'Why should I linger with a jerk like you?'

'I'm only giving you 1,500 baht for that, by the way.'

'That's fine by me,' she retorted. 'I am ready to get the hell out of here.'

It was such a shame, because he was staying in a very fancy hotel, and had appeared to be a nice guy at first.

During my first year at Patpong I was occasionally bought by Japanese men. It seemed that they gradually became more savvy and were tired of spending a lot more money for less hanky-panky in Thaniya, and so made their way to Patpong.

I took comfort from the fact that I had some experience in dealing with them, but my Japanese had gotten rusty over the years, although I still retained the essentials.

When I wanted to offer myself I would say, '*Yaritai desuka?*' and then state my price for a quickie, 'Give me *nisen o kane* baht *shotto.*'

I was going out to Khao San Road once with a young, skinny Japanese man who could speak some English. We wanted to go back to his hotel so we could finish our business there, but he couldn't remember where it was. He put his backpack on the street, and I looked in it for his hotel's business card, which would have the address on it. Just as he found it in his pocket, a police officer walked over to me and told me to give him my ID card. I reluctantly gave it to him and he took one look at me before telling me to collect my ID card at the police station. My first thought was that he was going to fine me for soliciting, so I asked my client to say that I was his girlfriend, not his prostitute.

When we arrived at the police station I found a line of streetwalkers sitting with their heads low, concealing their faces. It turned out I didn't need his false alibi after all. I was informed that I would be fined 100 baht for loitering. I instantly paid the fine and got my card back; it's not worth arguing with the police. The streetwalkers were all fined with the same charge. They are the easiest prey for the police, who want to make some quick money.

Later on we made our way to his hotel, where he invited me to his room. Once I was naked he asked me to lie down and took out a pink vibrator. He starting using it on my breasts, thighs, and around my vagina. The sensation tickled me and I couldn't hold my laughter in. He asked why I didn't like it, as women in the videos seemed to enjoy the gadget very much. I told him that in truth, those women were probably faking it. He seemed slightly disappointed, but responded by asking if I could give him oral sex. I happily obliged because he had a rather small penis. I put the condom on him and pleasured him for about five minutes before he penetrated me. He was so small that I almost couldn't feel his penis inside of me. He watched a porn movie throughout our intercourse, and I couldn't have cared less that he paid more attention to the girl in the video than to me. He worked himself up, and I faked moaning to help the poor man reach his climax faster. What I always fondly remember is that our encounter was less than 15 minutes in total, and he paid me my usual fee.

On the other end of the spectrum, I have also had men buy me out who have been simply too large for me to handle.

I had only been working in the bar for about two months when Nhim told me there was a client who wanted me to sit with him. At first I was delighted at the prospect of making some money. I wanted to buy a new mattress and clothes for Atid and Peung, who were growing so fast. Peung was a little doll to me and I loved dressing her up. My smile dimmed a little when I walked over to my prospective client. He was a

very muscular man of over six feet. Although he
appeared to be friendly and was generous with
money, I was reluctant and about to go back on
the stage when Nhim noticed my nerves and
told me to relax. She said I should treat him
as I would treat any client, as he had given me
no reason to disrespect him. Despite my gut
feeling, I agreed to leave the bar with him.

While he was in the shower I realised what
had perturbed me. He was a black man, and I
had heard stories about the size of their penises,
but I wasn't sure I believed that they were so big,
until this moment. His aroused penis resembled
a very large tube of toothpaste. I was frightened
by the size of it; that he would block my air
passage and I wouldn't be able to breathe if he
forced me to smoke it.

I was considering making a run for it when
he grabbed my wrist with his giant hand and
dragged me to the bed. He sat at the end of the
bed, and before I showed any sign of resistance,
he pushed my head against his erect penis. I
would never blow a man without him wearing a
condom, but I didn't get a chance to ask him to
put one on, as his penis was already in front of
my mouth. That suddenly sent tears streaming
down my face. As he was poking his penis at my
mouth, I kept my lips shut as tightly as I could
whilst sobbing and shaking.

His friendly manner was gone, and now he had a crazy grin on his face as he tried to invade my mouth. I was paralysed by fear and didn't know what to do. I just closed my eyes as if to fool myself that it was only a nightmare, and that when I opened my eyes again it would be over. I couldn't run for fear that he would hurt me. With both of his hands behind my head, he continued pushing my head against his penis, which was so hard and big that it hurt my face as he slapped it against my mouth. This made every hair of my body stand up, as it reminded me of the terror I experienced at the hands of Yuth. I was feeling more helpless than I'd ever felt before, and I couldn't summon enough strength to tell him to stop.

After what seemed to be an eternity, he realised he couldn't force me to perform oral sex. He let go of my head, and I almost fell back from his grasp. Then I broke down and cried uncontrollably. He threw my clothes at me and I dressed as quickly as I could and ran out of his room. I went straight to the bathroom in the lobby and washed my face thoroughly before rushing out of the hotel. I wondered if anyone would notice the humiliation on my face.

I needed someone to comfort me, so I went back to the bar. Nhim listened to my story and told me that she was sorry for pairing me up with him. I told her if a black man ever showed an interest in me again, she could tell him I was sick, or any excuse she could think of. I knew my limitations. I didn't tell Yuth about what happened because I knew he wouldn't sympathise.

I was quite shaken by the aggressive way in which this man had tried to get a blow job, and I stopped working for two days before the need of my family forced me to resume.

I told the story to Roj, who responded with two stories her own experiences with black clients, of which both had been positive. She told me that her clients were gentlemen who paid handsomely for her time, and understood that their endowments were too big for her. They just asked her to dance for them while they masturbated themselves. She tried to console me and made light of my horrible experience, saying I was just tremendously unlucky and I should make merit to prevent bad things from happening to me again.

After that, I always *wai*'d the shelf of deities situated in my bar every time I went out with a client, asking them to protect me. I also started dropping a small amount of alcohol onto the landing where my friends and I gathered, as a way to invite the spirits within the building to join us and watch over us.

My life continued as usual after that. Every evening we exchanged story after story about customers we had been with before work. The more I listened to other girls' client stories the more I couldn't help but feel lucky by comparison. Priew brought up a story of a client who was the same age as her grandfather. He asked her to tightly wind a thin nylon rope around the base of his scrotum because he couldn't maintain an erection. He then asked her to squeeze his balls hard while he masturbated.

Roj tried to top Priew with her latest client who had ejaculated on her face. Priew then responded with a girl she knew who ran away from her client because he wanted to push his fist up her ass. This story drew our loudest shrieks of disgust and terror.

I had once met a guy who liked to be poked by toothpicks on his sensitive area while he gratified himself. This was an easy job for me. Another girl said she knew someone who ate a customer's faeces. I recoiled in horror, as no amount of money in the world would make me do such an act.

There are pros and cons with each kind of man, but in general, we all agreed that *farang*s treated us with respect and spent their money generously, unlike their Thai counterparts who looked down on us and were often mean. Thai men were always a prostitute's last resort because they only paid between 500 to 1,000 baht for a short time. I never slept with Thai clients for this reason.

Although my friends tried to make light of these stories, there were times when I wished I was somewhere or someone else. Between each story there was this silence when I, or perhaps we, started to realise how horrible and abusive our clients could be and how much these 'funny' stories really affected us.

Despite how much I hate what I do, I can't imagine working anywhere but Patpong. Outside of here, there are only low-paid jobs available to a poorly educated girl like me. This place can be heaven or hell depending on what side of the fence you are on. The *farang*s who frequent this red-light district claim that it is like a utopian parallel universe. Whereas the prostitutes who work here see it as their own personal hell. Despair, betrayal, secrecy, and abuse lurk around every corner for us. No one is to be trusted in Patpong—be they prostitutes or *farang*s.

CHAPTER 11

WHEN I FIRST started out in the industry, I tried to look at prostitution objectively as a profession which didn't require any qualifications yet earned me quite a lot of money. My lack of education and experience disqualified me from other careers, aside from those involving menial, badly paid labour. All I needed to become a prostitute was a willingness to sell my body to strangers and an ability to keep the psychological effects of such a sale buried deep.

Of course, this was easier said than done, and I found that the longer I bottled up my emotions, the more they gnawed at my insides and threatened to claw their way to the surface. I couldn't talk to my family, and Yuth and I rarely talked at all anymore, never mind about our feelings. Most of the other girls in the bar could obviously identify with my situation, but

I found that, in general, when we talked about what we did for a living, there was a tendency to make light of it and laugh and giggle inanely as if it were all just one big joke. But the laughter often rang hollow and was quickly followed by an uncomfortable silence.

A little over a year ago, my tendency to try and ignore the seriousness of situations cost me dearly. The bar had been unusually quiet for a number of weeks, and I found myself short of money. Out of desperation I was forced to borrow from a Thai-Chinese moneylender. The moneylender in question was known as the 'mafia woman', and she was notorious in Bangkok. She was escorted at all times by several tall, burly bodyguards, and she had connections with a police officer which made her virtually untouchable. Despite her small stature, she was a tough, fearless-looking woman. Her hair was short and spiked, and she talked like a man, her vocabulary littered with expletives and threatening language. Rumour had it that most employees in the Patpong red-light district were in debt to her. These employees generally had no dealings with banks, as they rarely accumulated enough cash to give them reason to open up an account—so who else could they borrow from? Most of the prostitutes and doormen sent the best part of their monthly wage home to their family, and so they often ran out of money halfway through the month. They would then be forced to borrow short-term loans at high rates of interest.

So when I ran out of money myself one month, I asked one of the girls in the bar to introduce me to the mafia woman. The girl in question was in debt by a few thousand baht, but she didn't seem too worried about it. The mafia woman was greatly feared by many, but I had never actually heard any stories of her being violent, so I wasn't too worried about taking the money from her. She lent me the modest sum of 2,000 baht, and we agreed on a fee of 400 baht in interest. I was to repay her in instalments over the course of several weeks.

While I was still making these repayments, Yuth and I had a huge row. This wasn't very unusual in itself, only that this one was accompanied by a particularly severe beating that caused me to run away from home for two months. During this time I stayed with my mother and stopped working, so I ran myself into further debt. I still owed the moneylender 700 baht when I returned to Bangkok, but I foolishly thought that, this being quite a small sum of money, she would probably forget all about it. Perhaps Yuth had beaten me up one too many times because I certainly wasn't thinking straight.

Months passed by, and I forgot all about the money. No receipts had been printed or contracts signed—all I'd been given was a scrap of paper with the sum of money written on it, and I had lost that long ago. Then one Sunday night the mafia woman approached me outside the bar when I was on my way home. She was accompanied by her henchmen, and they all stared at me threateningly. I felt like a trapped animal. I told her that I was aware that I still owed her 700 baht. I had 500 baht in my pocket—my earnings from that night. I had intended on adding this 500 baht to Atid's and Peung's education fund but I offered it to the mafia woman with a sinking heart. But to my surprise she raised her hand to signal that it was too late for that. She informed me that I had accrued several months of interest, bringing my new debt up to 4,000 baht.

'The interest can't possibly be that high. I can't afford that kind of money,' I cried in shock.

'Well I suggest you find the money or I'll be forced to make an example of you.'

The alcohol pumping through my veins was all that kept my knees from buckling. I couldn't possibly afford that kind of money. I had no alternative but to sacrifice my dignity and plead with her to accept less. She knew that I had a young family to support, so I prayed that she might show me some mercy.

'Please, I can't possibly afford 4,000 baht. Will you accept 2,000 baht and my humble apologies for the delay? I had some family troubles, but these have all been taken care of.'

She stared at me coolly. Then, to my astonishment, she informed me that she would accept 2,000 baht but that she would come looking for me again in a couple of days. I wasn't sure if I could get the money together by then, but I was just relieved to have bought myself some time. The mafia woman and her thugs turned on their heels and made their way back down the street.

I got home that night to find Yuth drunk, unsurprisingly, and passed out on the couch, so even if I'd wanted to tell him about my 'meeting' I couldn't. There wouldn't have been much point anyway because, short of robbing a bank, there was nothing he could do. I crawled into bed praying that a *farang* would buy me the following night, and I would be able to settle my debt with the mafia woman.

Unfortunately, the following night was sluggish, and despite my best efforts I failed to attract the attention of a *farang*. I only earned 500 baht for the whole night on drinks commission. Just before closing time the moneylender appeared at my side. She smiled sweetly at me and asked me how I was. I *wai*'d her and in a half-whisper I told her that I could repay her only 500 of the 2,000 baht debt. She gasped in horror, as though I had just slapped her across the face.

'I'm not fucking accepting that.' In a low, threatening voice she continued, 'I think you need to step outside with me to discuss this matter further.'

She stalked off as I went to get changed, very slowly, into my clothes. I was hoping that if I took long enough she might grow tired of waiting for me and leave. As I made my way towards the exit, Roj, who had just returned from a client's hotel, stopped to warn me that the moneylender was waiting for me outside with two big bodyguards. She advised me to stay where I was. I decided to sit awhile with the *mamasan* while she was totting up the accounts for the night, but I knew I was only buying myself some time and that I couldn't sit there forever. It also crossed my mind that the later I got home the greater the chances were of Yuth rewarding me with a few slaps, kicks, and punches.

I rummaged in my purse and found an extra few hundred baht. I hoped that the mafia lady might accept a partial payment and allow me to settle the balance over the next few days. Besides, the streets were still quite busy, so I reasoned that she wouldn't want to beat me up in front of a crowd of people. The alcohol in my system clouded my judgement and fooled me into thinking that the situation wasn't all that bad. So I gathered my money together and left the safety of the bar. I walked towards them with one arm outstretched and my hand clutching the small bundle of notes. The mafia woman ignored the money and instead swung her two arms in my direction. She grabbed hold of my hair with one hand so as to hold my head steady, while her other hand, which was balled into a fist, slammed into me with tremendous velocity. The force of the punch sent me reeling, and my money flew up into the air. I fell to the ground as the bundle of notes rained down on me. But the mafia woman wasn't finished with me yet. She threw herself on top of me with a high-pitched war cry and started pounding my chest and head as hard as she could. She managed to get herself into a kneeling position and pinned my right arm to the ground with her knee while she continued to punch me. I threw a few feeble punches with my left arm, but they barely even made contact.

In the midst of this barrage of violence I became vaguely aware that a crowd had begun to assemble around us. But her assistants had formed a protective barrier and were warning people not to get involved.

'Stay out of this! One on one.'

The realisation that nobody was going to be allowed to intervene killed what little strength I had left. I let my body go limp with submission. As soon as I stopped fighting back the mafia woman seemed to lose interest and quickly got up. The beating had probably lasted only five minutes, but I knew that it was intended as a warning—a taste of things to come if I didn't repay my debt.

The mafia woman dusted herself off in an uncharacteristically ladylike manner, as if to suggest that this type of behaviour was normally beneath her, but that I had dragged her down to my base level. She rejoined her henchmen and they headed down the street. Perhaps it was because their backs were now turned to me that I was overcome by a sudden surge of courage. I scrambled to my feet and started to run after them. But my *mamasan*, who had been standing nearby, grabbed hold of me and pulled me back.

'Stop Bua! That's enough.'

'Enough? What do you mean enough? I'm going to make her pay for this.'

Nhim recommended that I go to the police instead. 'There are laws in this country against this sort of thing. Don't let her get away with it.'

There was a police kiosk at the end of the street, and I shakily made my way towards it. En route, two white men approached me and asked if I was okay; apparently they had tried to come to my defence, but the mafia woman's goons had made sure they got nowhere near me. I knew I probably looked terrible: my upper lip was cut and swollen, my chest felt heavy and bruised, and my right elbow was badly grazed from being pressed into the ground. Nevertheless, I managed to smile at the boys and assure them that I was fine. The two *farang*s showed much more concern about my well-being than the two policemen I spoke to at the kiosk. They were completely disinterested. The mafia woman had broken two laws: one, she was an illegal moneylender and two, she had just viciously attacked me in public. I begged the policemen to return to the bar with me so that they could interview the witnesses, but I was told that they couldn't do anything for me and that I should go to the nearest police station to file a complaint. They knew as well as I did that it would be a waste of time—the law caters only for rich Thais and foreigners.

I turned away from the kiosk, a heavy sense of injustice bearing down on me. I was about to go home when I bumped into a girl from the bar who told me that Aree, a well-respected *mamasan*, was looking for me. She managed another go-go bar in Patpong.

I broke down in floods of tears when I saw Aree. I don't think I've ever felt so alone and helpless before in my life. I had no one I could turn to—I couldn't ask my family for money, as it would have aroused too much suspicion surrounding my job, and then there was Yuth who had absolutely no money of his own and depended on me for every baht he spent. Aree asked me what had happened, and I told her my sorry story from beginning to end. She had worked as a dancer in the past, so she could empathise with me. As a *mamasan* she could be quite severe if a girl wasn't pulling her weight— she had been known to administer some harsh verbal abuse in her time. But ultimately she was a good person, and she proved this by taking 1,500 baht from her purse and beckoning to her doorman. She told him to go after the moneylender and give her the money in my name. I tried to thank her, but the words caught in my throat. She waved me off as if her gesture had been minuscule and didn't warrant a fuss.

'It's nothing dear. Just be more careful in the future.'

It was after 3am when I got home. Yuth opened the door to me, his mouth contorted into an ugly snarl. I had broken my curfew and he clearly intended to express his disappointment with me. But when he saw my face he gasped in horror. Yuth usually concentrated his attacks on my lower body, and he had become quite adept at minimising bruising, so the sight of my swollen and bloodied face shocked him. I rarely, if ever, cried in front of him, but the evening's events washed over me all at once, and the floodgates opened. Yuth wasn't quite sure what to say—he simply repeated over and over again that I had to give up prostitution, yet when I asked him how we would survive, he had no answer to give me. If Yuth had had a job then I would never have had to borrow money in the first place, I thought to myself. And if he hadn't beaten me so badly a few months ago, I wouldn't have run away and missed my loan repayments.

Yuth bathed my wounds and helped me to bed. I knew his tenderness stemmed from guilt and that tonight's bruises would soon be replaced by new injuries of his own infliction, but I still couldn't help but feel grateful to him for any little bit of kindness, however insincere.

When I arrived in the bar the following night, I found that news of the fight had spread like wildfire, and all eyes were on me. Some of the girls came up and asked me how I was. My face was still quite bruised and swollen, but I had layered on inches of make-up in an effort to cover it up. The aches and pains all over my body were a different matter, though, and there was no way of lessening their severity.

Later on in the night, as I was talking to a customer, a man came over and asked me if my name was Bua. I nodded, and he told me that the owner of the bar was waiting to speak to me in the office. I was immediately apprehensive— it was unusual for the owner to request such a meeting. I turned to the customer and excused myself, then changed out of my uniform and hurried up the street.

Word of my fight had clearly reached the boss, and when he saw my cut lip he asked me what had happened. I told him all about the loan, the inflated interest rates, and my eventual public humiliation at the hands of the mafia woman.

'What? Do you mean to tell me that not one person tried to stop her? Not one bouncer? Not one doorman?'

'Nobody helped me, they weren't allowed to. I heard her men warn everybody to stay away.'

I told him about the policemen and their complete lack of interest.

'Those sons of bitches! I'll drag their lazy asses down here. Nobody treats my girls like this!'

As he saw it, the mafia woman and her henchmen were flexing their muscles on his territory. He wasn't going to let them put one of his girls out of work. I wasn't sure whether his concern was personal or business-related, but to be honest, I didn't care what his motivation was—I was grateful either way. He told me to go back to work and that he would take care of the mafia woman.

I don't know what he did, but I never heard from her again.

CHAPTER 12

WHEREAS EVERY STEP I took in life led me to the red-light district of Patpong and further entrenched me in the sex industry, my sister Nang seemed destined for great things from the beginning. Education was the difference. She excelled at school and went on to get a degree in college. Her well-paid job in a law firm enabled her to buy a small house in Rangsit, a pleasant suburb of Bangkok. She generously invited mae and Geng to live with her, which meant that I got to see my eldest son much more frequently.

Then one day several years ago, my sister met a Norwegian man called Oddveig while he was on holiday in Thailand. At the end of his stay, they decided to keep in contact by email until, several months and many emails later, Oddveig returned. They were so in love that they couldn't bear to be separated again, so they decided to get married.

Their wedding day was a happy one for all the family. My father even turned up, alone, although he was careful to stay out of my mother's way. The part-Buddhist, part-western ceremony took place in my sister's house in Rangsit; it wasn't big enough for the 70 guests in attendance, so the party spilled out onto the street. Nang wore a beautiful white wedding dress while Oddveig wore a smart, dark suit.

I was genuinely happy for Nang, but as memories surfaced of my own pitiful ceremony with Chai, I couldn't help but compare our fortunes. Educated and independent, my sister didn't need a farang to rescue her, and yet one had come to take her to Norway while I remained stuck in Patpong with an abusive partner.

As tempting as it is to paint her life as a fairy tale, I know Pang has faced her share of difficulties. Oddveig is a widower with grown children who could not immediately accept their father's new wife. She also found it difficult to adjust to life in Norway. Her one stipulation before moving was that she be allowed to continue working, as she was desperate to retain a sense of independence. She was also keen to dispel the stereotype that Thai women marry westerners purely for their money. Although Oddveig was initially against the idea, he eventually relented, and Nang now works as a nurse in a retirement home, which she finds very rewarding. In her spare time, she moonlights as a matchmaker and has already successfully set up two of her friends with Norwegian men. I can't help but find a small amount of irony in the fact that my sister and I are operating at completely opposite ends of the scale—whereas Nang is offering a service to help men find true love, I provide them with fast, no-strings-attached pleasure.

Nang's good fortune was beneficial to the whole family. It is usual for Thai people to inundate a successful member of the family with requests for money, no matter how distant the relative. Our family is no exception, but Nang has remained unendingly generous. Some years ago she loaned my brother Nop 60,000 baht with which to buy a van. He was supposed to pay for it in instalments, but Nang soon discovered our brother takes after *mae* in his inability to manage money.

Unfortunately, it's not just money given to him that he squanders. Because he was the only member of my family in Thailand to have a bank account, Nang had trusted him and would often transfer money with instructions to pass it on to me. But time and time again, Nop would conveniently 'forget', and by the time I found out about it, it was usually long gone.

Occasionally, my sister has to say no to the never-ending requests for money—if she didn't, she'd end up going hungry herself. But she can never turn down a family member seeking help to get an education. She has generously contributed money towards the schooling of my eldest child Geng. Sadly, he is not very academic. When he started missing school a few months ago, Nang rang him from Norway to lecture him about the importance of finishing school. Nang and I are well aware of the value of education—I serve as a daily reminder for both of us.

Because Geng was raised by *mae*, he sees me more as a big sister than a mother. I try not to let it bother me and instead focus on the advantages of our relationship. For example, I am privy to personal details of his life that mothers are generally excluded from. He recently rang to tell me that he and his girlfriend had recently had unprotected sex and they were now worried that she might be pregnant. He knew I wouldn't get angry with him but would instead offer him practical advice. I told him that condoms were on sale in his local 7-11 shop and to go buy some immediately. Thankfully, it turned out to be a false alarm. I dearly want him to finish school and continue on to college so he can get a good job and be able to support his family when the time comes.

Chai continues to send money to my mother for Geng's upkeep, but he and Geng have no contact with one another. At times I feel guilty that Geng grew up without his father in his life, but unlike Yuth, Chai never showed any paternal instincts, and I always feared that it would only be a matter of time before Geng would fall prey to his violence. It was for Geng's protection, too, that he never came to live with Yuth and me. Although Yuth takes very good care of his own children and would never do anything to harm them, Geng is not his son, and his safety could not be guaranteed.

As for Peung and Atid, they are still quite young but they both seem very bright and enjoy school immensely. I take great pleasure in buying them the various books, stationery and other equipment necessary for school. Whatever they need, I make sure that they have it. My own abiding memories of my education centre on my family's poverty and the constant struggle to afford such basic necessities as text books and school bags.

The other day I asked Atid what he wants to be when he grows up. He told me that he wants to be a police officer because he likes the uniform. He then pulled me closer and whispered in my ear that he would also then be able to arrest his father. At this I felt my eyes well up with tears. I know that he and Peung must be very confused by their father's two starkly contrasting personalities. Yuth is very kind and affectionate towards them and they love him dearly, but when they see me walking with a limp or wincing with pain at the slightest movement, they know who is responsible for the injuries.

After my sister settled into married life in Norway, she offered me a means of escape. She suggested that I live with her and Oddveig for a while. Wages for waitressing or bar work were much higher in Norway than in Thailand, and I would finally be able to earn some decent money without having to suffer from regular beatings. It seemed too good to be true, and it was. Yuth wouldn't hear of it. I think he feared that if I left I would never return, and he would never have let me take the children with me. If I didn't see with my own eyes how tender he is with them, I wouldn't believe him capable of affection anymore.

But I know how attached my children are to their father, and it is for this reason that I have stayed with him, even if it means living under the constant threat of violence. If I took them away, they would eventually come to resent me. My children will have their father, and they will have the means and the encouragement necessary to pursue an education.

Still I worry that even though I have done everything in my power to ensure my children are materially better off than I was as a child, perhaps I have failed them emotionally. I don't get to kiss them goodnight at bedtime or listen to their stories from the day over dinner. I don't see them nearly as much as I'd like to. I entered the nightmarish world of prostitution so that I could provide for them, yet I fear that I am sending them to sleep at night with a different type of hunger in their bellies.

EPILOGUE

To THIS DAY, I have never breathed a word of what I do to any member of my family for two important reasons. First, they would be horrified to learn that I have sex with strangers in exchange for money. And second, I think my parents would blame themselves for the course my life has taken, and they have enough to worry about without adding that burden. While *mae* has Geng to care for, *por* has discovered that he replaced *mae* with yet another woman addicted to gambling. His *mia* runs her own underground lottery system and takes bets from people in the neighbourhood. She's never able to pay the ones who strike lucky, so my father is obliged to pay out of his own pocket, an action he was already well-accustomed to.

I guess nobody intentionally sets out to repeat the same mistakes; some people just have a blind spot when it comes to certain dangers in life. I guess it's similar to my fleeing the abuse of Chai only to fall into the equally violent arms of Yuth.

There is a western saying, 'Time heals all wounds.' And while it's true that all the cuts and bruises I've received over the years have healed with the passage of time, the emotional scars are a different story. Every *farang* that I sleep with, every beating at the hands of Yuth, and every time I miss out on tucking my children into bed at night, another scar is added to my collection.

I have long since accepted that my dream of taking my children and fleeing Yuth will never be a reality. I will never be able to separate my children from their father.

I'm ashamed to say, however, that I haven't given up hope that someday a rich *farang* might come into my life and rescue me from prostitution. I don't even mind if he has another wife in his native country—so long as I can be honest with him about my children, I would settle for him just visiting me occasionally and sending me financial support. I don't think I'm asking for too much—I'll forsake the white picket fences just to escape the red-light district of Patpong.

My dream is fading fast, though—I am almost twice the age of some of the girls who dance in the bar and already that is too old for many *farang*s. I find myself lying about my age and even reducing my fee to attract more customers. What's next for me? Will my customers dwindle away until I'm eventually forced to participate in lewd sex shows in the upstairs bars of Patpong—shooting ping pong balls from my body for the entertainment of *farang*s?

I feel crippled by fear. I have been in this industry in one way or another for so long now that I know no other life. The red-light district of Patpong is no longer a place I visit only at night time; in my mind, it has spilled over into the daylight hours and has become enmeshed in every aspect of my life.

Any decisions I have made have always been with my family in mind. Perhaps they weren't always the best ones, but my only defence is that I made them with the best of intentions. My belief in reincarnation gives me the strength to go on. I see this life as just another chapter in a never-ending sequence of lives; perhaps this particular instalment doesn't have a happy ending, but I pray to Buddha that the sequel will be different.

AFTERWORD

DURING THE EARLY interviews with Miss Bangkok, I casually mentioned that she should come up with a pseudonym to be used in order to protect her privacy. She came back the next day with a broad smile on her face and announced proudly that she wanted to be called Bua Boonmee. She impressed me, and I agreed on the first hearing because the name is so simple and yet rings so Thai.

Little did we know how ironic her choice would become as her story unfolded.

A good Buddhist will know a thing or two about *bua* (lotus). Buddha himself classifies people into different kinds of *bua*. Lotus roots in mud but blossoms into a beautiful flower, thus, every individual has the ability to gain enlightenment and grow spiritually. The ones that blossom and surface will enjoy the sunlight.

The ones that remain in the mud on the river bed will lose themselves in the dark.

In keeping with this analogy, it's harsh but true to say that Bua is the lowest kind of lotus. She is lost in her predicament, and is unable to see her way to the surface.

Her fake surname *boon-mee* translates to 'having good fortune'. Only as I write this do I realise how painfully the fortune she hopes for contrasts with her reality.

More often than not Bua let her teardrops and bruises recount the latest heartbreak she endured, and beating she took as she stumbled for words. There were uncomfortable silences here and there.

But when she broke the silence, a fierceness often took its place as she talked about her abusers. I was always surprised at this transformation because Bua is usually a meek woman and, as a 'good' Thai woman, you shouldn't be angry or lose your temper.

She once looked me in the eyes and said, 'You must get this into the book. Promise me.' Squeezing a piece of paper towel as if it were the neck of her abusive husband, she wiped a tear away.

Telling the world about her misery is the only bitter revenge she'll ever get, I guess. As saddening and distressing as her story is, it's all the more reason it should be told. To be able to sit and talk with her was a sad privilege and an eye-opening experience for me as a Thai.

I'm proud that we kept our promises to her. Her life continues beyond this book into the unforeseen future, but at least she talked about one of the many elephants (in the room) Thailand blissfully ignores. She is brave to speak up.

Kob khun (Thank you), Bua, and to your friends, for sharing your stories in this book. From the bottom of my heart, I hope you are all well and safe.

- Pornchai Sereemongkonpol,
Maverick House Publishers,
SE Asia.

THE LAST EXECUTIONER

MEMOIRS OF THAILAND'S LAST PRISON EXECUTIONER

BY CHAVORET JARUBOON
WITH NICOLA PIERCE

Chavoret Jaruboon was personally responsible for executing 55 prison inmates on Thailand's infamous death row.

As a boy, he wanted to be a teacher like his father, then a rock'n'roll star like Elvis, but his life changed when he joined Thailand's prison service. From there he took on one of the hardest jobs in the world.

Honest and often disturbing—but told with surprising humour and emotion—*The Last Executioner* is the remarkable story of one man's experiences with life and death.

Emotional and at times confronting, the book grapples with the controversial topic of the death sentence and makes no easy reading.

This book is not for the faint-hearted—*The Last Executioner* takes you right behind the bars of the Bangkok Hilton and into death row.

'Not afraid to tell it like it is.' - IPS Asia

'A truly remarkable story.' - Manchester Weekly News

'Grisly, yet riveting reading.' - The Big Chilli, Thailand.

To order this book go to www.maverickhouse.com

LOOT

INSIDE THE WORLD OF STOLEN ART

BY THOMAS MCSHANE
WITH DARY MATERA

Thomas McShane is one of the world's foremost authorities on the art theft business. With great energy and imagination, *Loot* recounts some of his most thrilling cases as he matches wits with Mafia mobsters and smooth criminals.

Covering his 36 years as an FBI Agent, the author brings us on a thrilling ride through the underworld of stolen art and historical artefacts as he dons his many disguises and aliases to chase down $900 million worth of stolen art pieces.

McShane has worked on high profile cases all over the world, including the Beit heist in Ireland. From Rembrandts robbed in Paris to van Goghs vanishing in New York, McShane's tale is one of great adventure, told with surprising humour.

The Thomas Crown Affair meets *Donnie Brasco* in this story of a truly extraordinary life.

To order this book go to www.maverickhouse.com

MORE NON-FICTION FROM MAVERICK HOUSE

WELCOME TO HELL

ONE MAN'S FIGHT FOR LIFE INSIDE THE 'BANGKOK HILTON'

BY COLIN MARTIN

Written from his cell and smuggled out page by page, Colin Martin's autobiography chronicles an innocent man's struggle to survive inside one of the world's most dangerous prisons.

After being swindled out of a fortune, Martin was let down by the hopelessly corrupt Thai police. Forced to rely upon his own resources, he tracked down the man who conned him and, drawn into a fight, accidentally stabbed and killed the man's bodyguard.

Martin was arrested, denied a fair trial, convicted of murder and thrown into prison—where he remained for eight years. Honest and often disturbing, *Welcome to Hell* is the remarkable story of how Martin was denied justice again and again.

In his extraordinary account, he describes the swindle, his arrest and vicious torture by police, the unfair trial, and the eight years of brutality and squalor he was forced to endure.

To order this book go to www.maverickhouse.com

NOT ON OUR WATCH

By DON CHEADLE
AND JOHN PRENDERGAST

If you care about issues of genocide and other mass atrocities, and you truly want to make a difference, this book was written for you.

The brutality of civil war in places like Sudan, Northern Uganda, Congo, and Somalia seems far away and impossible to solve. Six million graves have been freshly dug during the last couple of decades in this modern-day holocaust, and many millions of people have been driven from their homes.

Angered by the devastating violence that has engulfed Darfur and other war zones in Africa, famed actor Don Cheadle teamed up with leading human-rights activist John Prendergast to shine a haunting spotlight on these atrocities. Here, they candidly reveal heart-wrenching personal accounts of their experiences visiting Darfur and Northern Uganda.

The book outlines six inspiring strategies that every one of us can adopt to help bring about change. No personal action is too small. For the sanctity of the human race, it is imperative that we not stand idly by as innocent civilians.

Take a stand. Raise your voice. Find out how *you* can make a difference. The time to act is now.

'A compelling account of the gravest humanitarian crisis of our time.' - Martin Bell, UNICEF Ambassador.

FARANG

By Dr Iain Corness

Dr Iain Corness fell in love with Thailand on a holiday in 1975, and finally managed to move there permanently in 1997. As a settled farang, or foreigner, he enjoys a unique perspective on Thai life and all its eccentricities; looking in from the outside while also getting to see the things most foreigners don't.

His stories and anecdotes are full of the joys of life, and celebrate this exotic and exciting land in all its glory with painfully funny observations. From a date with a fortune teller to tales of a reincarnated squid, Corness revels in the chaos and charm of 'the only country where you can be run over by a shop.'

This is a book to be enjoyed by tourists and Thais alike.

Not only does Dr Iain see the things that make up Thailand, but he experiences them as well, bringing up unseen aspects and presenting them to the reader in a very humorous way. - Chiangmai Mail

To order this book go to www.maverickhouse.com

NIGHTMARE IN LAOS

By KAY DANES

Hours after her husband Kerry was kidnapped by the Communist Laos government, Kay Danes tried to flee to Thailand with her two youngest children, only to be intercepted at the border.

Torn away from them and sent to an undisclosed location, it was then that the nightmare really began. Forced to endure 10 months of outrageous injustice and corruption, she and her husband fought for their freedom from behind the filth and squalor of one of Laos' secret gulags.

Battling against a corrupt regime, she came to realise that there were many people worse off held captive in Laos—people without a voice, or any hope of freedom. Kay had to draw from the strength and spirit of those around her in order to survive this hidden hell, while the world media and Australian government tried desperately to have her and Kerry freed before it was too late and all hope was lost.

For Kay, the sorrow and pain she saw people suffer at the hands of the regime in Laos, where human rights are non-existent, will stay with her forever, and she vowed to tell the world what she has seen. This is her remarkable story.

To order this book go to www.maverickhouse.com

THE MIRACLE OF FATIMA MANSIONS

AN ESCAPE FROM DRUG ADDICTION

BY SHAY BYRNE

The Miracle of Fatima Mansions is the moving story of a teenage boy who lost himself to drug addiction after the death of his father.

Set against the backdrop of working-class Dublin in the 1970s, Shay Byrne has written a brutally honest account of his addiction, his crimes and his redemption.

Byrne narrowly escaped death during a violent attack at Fatima Mansions, the flat complex synonymous with extreme social depravation, social decay and drugs. It was the unlikely location of an epiphany that would transform his life.

The incident forced Byrne to confront his inner demons and seek help at a radical treatment centre.

Told with searing honesty, Byrne's debut book is the most insightful, candid and thought-provoking book ever written on Dublin's drug culture. It is destined to become a classic.

To order this book go to www.maverickhouse.com

BLOOD AND MONEY

By DAVE COPELAND

Filled with paranoid mobsters, clever scams, and deep betrayals, *Blood and Money* gives a unique insight into one of the most successful gangs ever to operate on American soil.

By the time Ron Gonen arrived in New York City he had broken out of prison in Germany, been exiled from Israel, fled England as a prime suspect in a multi-million dollar crime ring, and had been chased out of Guatemala. Gonen lived life in the fast lane until things spiralled out of control.

In the 1980s, a small group of Israeli nationals set up one of the most lucrative crime syndicates in New York City's history. With rackets ranging from drug dealing to contract killings, their crime spree was so violent that it wasn't long before they were dubbed the 'Israeli Mafia'.

The gang went to war with the Italian mafia, killed Russian gangsters and pulled off the biggest gold heist in the history of Manhattan's Diamond District.

They would have become the most powerful gang in the New York underworld had Gonen not decided to risk his life and become an FBI informant. *Blood and Money* is his story.

'A thrilling guts-and-glory look inside the Israeli organised crime machine of 1980s New York City.' - Publishers Weekly

To order this book go to www.maverickhouse.com